NETWORK

...

NETWORK

The Right People... In the Right Places...
For the Right Reasons

IMPLEMENTATION GUIDE

Bruce Bugbee · Don Cousins · Bill Hybels

ZondervanPublishingHouse
Grand Rapids, Michigan

A Division of HarperCollinsPublishers

WILLOW CREEK RESOURCES

Network: Implementation Guide
Copyright ©1994 by Willow Creek Community Church

Requests for information should be addressed to:
Zondervan Publishing House Grand Rapids, Michigan 49530

Edited by Jack Kuhatschek and Rachel Boers
Cover design by John M. Lucas
Interior design by Paetzold Design

ISBN 0-310-43261-8

94 / 95 / 96 / 97 / 98 /   / 7 / 6 / 5 / 4 / 3 / 2 /

TO VALERIE

For the many years
she has so faithfully served
me and our four children:
Brittany, Brianne, Bronwyn, and Todd.

CONTENTS

FOREWORD

I consider the development of the Network materials to be one of the most significant breakthroughs in the history of Willow Creek Community Church.

We discovered years ago that believers flourish in their service to Christ when they are serving in the area of their giftedness and in conjunction with their God-given uniqueness. The Network materials grew out of our desire to help believers discover their spiritual gifts, and then determine where to use them in our church body.

The results of Network have been astounding. Imagine having fresh servants entering the work force of the church every year, confident of their giftedness and eager to invest them in service for God's glory.

It is happening!

May God bless you as you learn and grow through these tremendous materials.

Bill Hybels
Senior Pastor
Willow Creek Community Church

ACKNOWLEDGMENTS

It has been said that "there is nothing new under the sun" (Ecclesiastes 1:9). These Network materials bear witness to that timeless truth.

I have attempted to put together a simple and easy-to-walk-through process for believers who desire to serve in the local church. In doing so I have utilized the insights of many authors, teachers, leaders, and servants. This material has been adapted, edited, and written to present a comprehensive and consistent approach for those who desire to do ministry. But it could not have been done without the input and assistance of many people.

Peter Wagner's vision inspired me to see Spiritual Gifts understood, discovered, and used in ministry. His excellent seminar materials laid a foundation for my thinking.

Jolene Frazier has demonstrated warmth and grace in her service and development of the Network Team.

Ron and Bonnie Ek, Curt Mueller, Bob Brown, Clyde Ericson, Bill Marquardt and so many others have been grand encouragers for me and the body of Christ.

Wendy Guthrie has made comprehensive contributions to the interactive learning that is now a part of Network. Her commitment to quality communication and biblical truth will benefit each participant. She has been a gracious project manager in the development of this new format.

John Nixdorf brought training expertise and perspective to the rewriting process. His patient and persistent spirit made an otherwise tedious task fun and meaningful.

Jim Mellado served as the catalyst to move the existing materials into this new international phase. He had started a Network Ministry and shares the passion and vision for what God is doing through the Network process.

I appreciate the Willow Creek Association[SM] for its support and assistance in making these materials available to even greater numbers of believers. Their conferences have provided many exciting opportunities to present Network to Christian leaders around the world.

And a special thanks to those who have participated in Network at Willow Creek Community Church. Your feedback and support have freed me to be more faithful and diligent in my own service to the body of Christ.

To all these people, and the many others who are so faithfully using their gifts, thank you. Together, we can serve yet a greater body of believers who want their lives to count for Christ and impact the world for which he died.

Bruce Bugbee
President
Network Ministries International

INTRODUCTION

This Implementation Guide is simply a road map to implementing the Network Process in your church. As with most maps, there are alternate routes you can take on the way to your destination.

The Network Process uses multiple recruiting paths for greater impact. There are three doors of the church your Network Ministry needs to open:

1. The Front Door — Reaching those who have not served
2. The Side Door — Reaching those who are serving
3. The Back Door — Reaching those who used to serve

Consider an intentional and sensitive strategy for each. How will you target getting everyone?

REALITY CHECK #1: Making Network "mandatory" in order to serve will create resistance. There is this thing called "The People Factor." When we are told we "have to," there is something inside most of us that says "No, I won't." Challenge, encourage, share the values, communicate the benefits. Permit your people to seek out Network as the Holy Spirit prompts them.

REALITY CHECK #2: Network cannot meet all the recruiting needs of your church. Everyone in ministry should be seeking out those who might enjoy serving with them. There is an open chair in every ministry team. Prayerfully consider who God might be preparing to fill it. This kind of relational recruiting is a powerful and effective way of getting people started into ministry. At the appropriate time they should be directed to Network to help them better understand who God has made them to be and where they might best make their unique contribution.

Your church is unique. You have a history and purpose. There are individual and corporate dynamics involved. While each church implementing the Network Process is different, we are all clear on the goal: to have fully devoted followers of Jesus Christ being fruitful and fulfilled, making their unique contribution in a meaningful place of service.

So, use this as a GUIDE. This is a map that will enable you to be effective in the development of your Network ministry. Make the appropriate adjustments that are necessary for its implementation in your church.

There are certain values that we are putting into practice. These shared values are behind the methodology used in this Implementation Guide. Feel free to modify the methods described here, but be careful not to lose Network's values.

By the end of this decade, you will be among those churches that have embraced the biblical vision and practical application of each believer actively participating in the life and ministry of the local church. It is time to network our Kingdom resources and be the church that Christ has called us to be.

There are uncommon blessings that await us.

Bruce Bugbee

OVERVIEW

This Implementation Guide is provided to help you install a fruitful Network ministry in your church.

The Implementation process has been broken into three phases:

- Phase 1: Senior Leadership Commitment

- Phase 2: Ministry Preparation

- Phase 3: Network Implementation

This guide concisely describes the actions recommended in each phase. Worksheets to assist your activities are provided in the appendix.

The natural tendency is to skip right to Phase 3, and start putting on Network Discovery sessions. If you do that, experience has shown that you may end up with *a* Network ministry, of sorts, but it will not be an *effective* Network ministry. Carefully work through each of the steps recommended in this guide.

Remember the clichè: "You never get a second chance to make a first impression." Invest the time to lay a firm foundation of support and understanding for the Network vision and process.

Senior Leadership Commitment

WHAT IS IT?

In this phase, the purpose is to get senior leadership to personally and organizationally commit to Network.

Personally commit
> As individuals, they have to experience the benefits of Network to them *personally*. They need to believe it is true, that it provides an accurate and healthy description of them, and that it makes sense. They must see the value to them personally before they can see the value of Network for the church.

Organizationally commit
> As leaders they need to believe that the *church* would benefit from Network and then commit to assisting the implementation process (i.e., commit their budget, staff, and facilities). They need to be willing to make *organizational* changes and adjustments.

Senior leadership consists of recognized decision-makers, stakeholders, and key influencers including: senior pastor, elders, deacons, board members, and key staff.

WHY IS IT IMPORTANT?

It is important to obtain senior leadership's *assistance* with the process by committing their energy and resources to Network (see "organizationally commit" above). Network is not another ministry in the church, it is the way to do church.

CAUTION

If you skip this phase and do not receive senior leadership's support, Network will not happen on a churchwide basis. People will begin to have an idea of where they should be serving, but the ministries will still try to "slot" them according to current ministry needs, not according to who God designed them to be. This will create confusion and resistance.

PHASE 1: SENIOR LEADERSHIP COMMITMENT

	Form A Network Team	Prepare The Network Proposal	Present The Network Proposal	Have Senior Leadership Personally Experience Network
Senior Leadership			• Participate in Network Proposal Presentation • Commit to experience Network personally	• Attend Network Discovery sessions • Participate in discussion of Consultation • Personally and organizationally commit to implementing Network
Network Team	• Identify others who will assist you • Share the vision of Network with these people • Have them experience Network • Obtain commitment	• Determine time to present proposal • List issues to address • Meet with senior leadership individually • Prepare responses to senior leaders' concerns • Write the proposal • Determine who will present the proposal	• Share the vision and values of Network • Present the Network Proposal • Ask for a commitment to experience Network personally	• Schedule and plan Network presentation • Select presenter • Conduct Network Discovery sessions • Discuss Consultation step • Discuss feedback and debrief the Discovery and Consultation steps • Ask for a decision on the part of senior church leadership: *Are you at a point where you can personally and organizationally commit to implementing Network at our church?*

STEP 1 FORM A NETWORK TEAM

Why?

To assist you in preparing and presenting the Network proposal to senior church leadership and in overseeing the implementation process.

How?

1. Identify others who will be able to assist you in:

- Drawing up a proposal for Network

- Presenting the proposal to senior leadership

- Overseeing the implementation of Network, including

    –implementing the Discovery Step

    – implementing the Consultation Step

    – implementing Information Support

    It is recommended that there be a point person for each of the above implementation areas. However, if you do not have three people on the Network Team, remember that these responsibilities still need to be accomplished and need to be divided between the number of people you do have. Recruit more than three people for the Network Team if possible.

The people you recruit for the Network Team should be able to help you prepare and present the Network proposal and oversee its implementation. They should also know some of the senior leadership so they will be able to talk with them personally about Network, and to identify concerns they might have to address in the Network proposal.

These people may or may not be in formal leadership positions in your church, but they still exercise influence. Also, the staff person who will oversee this team should be identified and included if he or she has not been already.

2. Share the vision of Network to these potential Network Team leaders.

- Show them the Network Vision and Consultant Training video

- Describe their potential roles (see the ministry position descriptions in the Appendix).

3. Have them experience Network if they haven't already.

> Your Network Team needs to be personally committed to Network. They should have a Passion for the Network Goal of "helping believers be fruitful and fulfilled in a meaningful place of service." They also need to be committed to the concept of educating and equipping followers of Christ for service based on each person's *Servant Profile*.

> A checklist is provided in the Appendix to use in planning the Discovery sessions.

4. Obtain their commitment to be on the Network Team.

> After you cast the vision for Network and have your prospective team experience it personally, assess whether they have a Passion and commitment for Network before you formally ask them to be on the Network Team. Also assess whether they have the gifts, experience, skills, and/or abilities to assist you with implementing the Network Process.

> Finally, keep in mind that this team will be working closely together, and it is important that they are able to work well together.

STEP 2 — PREPARE THE NETWORK PROPOSAL

Why?

To create understanding, credibility, and trust with the senior leadership.

How?

1. Determine a date, time, and location to present the Network Proposal to your church's senior leadership.

2. List the issues to address in the proposal.

> Your church leaders have many concerns. Concerns like building programs, operating expenses, pastoral care, staffing issues, church discipline, giving and tithing, teaching, volunteer recruitment, etc. To get the support of your leaders, you need to show how Network contributes to *solving* these concerns. Otherwise they may view Network as just another program to manage, rather than a part of the solution.

Specific issues to include in your Network Proposal are:

- What is Network? Include that Network is a comprehensive approach to service in the church. Present Network's vision, values, and benefits. Consider using the Network Vision and Consultant Training video to describe it (information on Network's vision and Consultant Training and values, benefits, the biblical truths accessed by Network, and why Network is unique are provided in the Appendix for your use in preparing your Network proposal).

- How does Network relate to your church's mission or vision statement?

- How does Network work? Include that Network is a proven process which can be used on an ongoing basis. Mention Network's three steps: Discovery, Consultation, and Service.

- What staffing will be required?

- What equipment will be needed (computer, software, etc.)?

- What publicity and communication will be done?

- What will it cost?

- How will Network be presented in your church (seminar, small group, new members class, Sunday School class, retreat, etc.)?

- Any other concerns particular to your church. Have those members of your Network Team who know members of your senior leadership identify issues of concern to those senior leaders. Identify specific questions that senior leadership may ask and concerns they may have, and prepare in advance to answer them. To help you, see Network Questions and Answers in the Appendix.

3. Meet with the senior leadership individually.

In a one-on-one setting, assess what each senior leader knows about Network, and what may be some perceptions or misconceptions. Attempt to identify issues and concerns about volunteer participation in the church or about Network. Remember, your purpose in these meetings is to *listen and understand* them, NOT to begin explaining or defending Network. You will be able to explain Network when you present your proposal.

It is wise to assess your church leaders' views *before* you formally present your proposal for approval. If your leaders have had time to think about Network, and had any questions or misconceptions dealt with in advance, the formal presentation will go much more smoothly. It is usually much easier to handle objections and questions on an individual basis than in a meeting.

After you have had these individual meetings, proceed to #4.

4. Write down the responses to those issues identified in #2 and #3 above. If there is no answer at this time, state in the Network Proposal that you are *aware* of the issues but you do not have a solution at this time.

5. Write the Network Proposal.

   As you prepare your proposal, keep in mind:

   • **Be Wise:** Who will be receiving this proposal? What kinds of questions will they ask? Attempt to "answer" their questions in your proposal.

   • **Be Brief:** Keep your proposal to one or two pages. Be concise and thorough. Touch all the bases to reflect your awareness of the issues and present your vision for its implementation.

   • **Be Excellent:** Your proposal should be well laid out and easy to follow. Be sure everyone has received the proposal in a timely fashion for prayerful reflection.

   A sample proposal and worksheets to help you organize your proposal are included in the Appendix.

6. Determine who will present the Network Proposal. If you want the Network Team to present it, determine who will present which portion.

STEP 3 PRESENT THE NETWORK PROPOSAL TO SENIOR LEADERSHIP

Why?

To get your senior leadership to commit to experience Network. Commitment of your church leadership is essential for successful Network implementation. You need more than just passive assent to the Network Process. You need their *personal* and *organizational* commitment. This can only come after they personally experience Network.

Senior leadership's commitment is essential. It will be difficult to get the support of the general membership of your church if the senior leadership lacks commitment to Network.

How?

1. Share the vision and values of Network using the Network vision video.

2. Present the Network Proposal.

3. Ask for a commitment to experience Network personally. Set a date and location.

Caution

If your senior leadership is not willing to experience Network, stop here. Take the time to find out what are their objections, and any issues that still need to be addressed.

STEP 4 HAVE LEADERSHIP PERSONALLY EXPERIENCE NETWORK

Why?

For senior leadership to personally and organizationally commit to Network.

If the senior pastor and the church's key influencers are not committed to Network, it will be very difficult for you to have a successful Network ministry.

That is why it is important for the senior pastor, staff, and senior leadership of your church to personally experience Network.

There is a big difference between an intellectual assent to the biblical concepts of Network and a true commitment to its practical application. Attending Network can help bridge that gap. When personally experienced, most adversaries become advocates.

Offer Network to your senior leadership and their spouses. While spouses may not be in formal leadership positions, these people are usually well tied into the *informal* structure of your church and can help the Network ministry with good "word of mouth" advertising. The format may be a retreat, weekend seminar, four-week program, or whatever fits your schedule. Indicate how each leader will personally benefit and be better equipped for their own ministry in the church.

NOTE: When you are together and ready to start Network, challenge everyone to take off their "leadership hats." Tell them: "This seminar is to be experienced as a believer seeking to better understand who God has made you to be. Don't be thinking about how this will work, or will have to be changed. Following the seminar, we will put our leadership hats back on and do a responsible analysis. This journey is for you!"

How?

1. Schedule and plan the Network presentation (location, date, time, breaks, etc.). Invite spouses if possible.

2. Select the presenter.

3. Conduct the Network Discovery sessions.

   At the beginning of the Discovery sessions, state your goal of obtaining leadership's personal and organizational commitment to implementing Network at your church. This will let your leadership know that you will be asking for a commitment at some point, so that when you do ask for a commitment, they are not taken by surprise.

4. Discuss the Consultation step.

   It is helpful to have your leaders get a feel for the Consultation. You have several options at this point:

   • Use the Network Vision and Consultant Training video to show selected portions of a consultation. Then discuss.

- Take a volunteer and do a quick "on the spot" consultation in front of the whole group. Sit on the platform and let the audience eavesdrop. Then discuss.

- Simply explain the purpose and format of the consultation. Demonstrate with a few sample *Servant Profiles* how that information can lead to some ministry possibilities. Then discuss.

5. Discuss feedback and debrief the Discovery and Consultation steps.

Sample questions to stimulate discussion:

- How did you personally benefit from this seminar?

- What insights did you gain from the process?

- How do you feel that others in our church could benefit from this process?

- How do you think this might make a difference in the vitality, ministry, and impact of our church?

- What do you see as the greatest obstacles and challenges facing our church in the implementation of Network?

6. Ask for a decision: "Are you at a point where you can personally and organizationally commit to implementing Network at our church?"

If the answer is yes, move to Phase 2: Ministry Preparation

If the answer is no, find out what the objections, reservations, and concerns are and address them.

IS YOUR SENIOR LEADERSHIP ON BOARD?

ARE THEY PERSONALLY AND ORGANIZATIONALLY COMMITTED?

Have You

❏ Formed a Network Team?

❏ Prepared the Network Proposal?

❏ Presented the Network Proposal?

❏ Had your church's senior leadership personally experience Network?

Each of these items is *critical* to the full success of Network in your church. Complete each item before proceeding with the implementation process.

Ministry Preparation

WHAT IS IT?

In this phase the ministries in your church are integrated into Network, and additional Network Team members are identified and trained.

Ministry leaders are integrated into Network.

It is important that ministry leaders understand and are committed to Network so they will begin recruiting people according to their *Servant Profile*. Their commitment is also needed so they will commit the time and effort necessary to create Network ministry position descriptions.

Additional Network Team members are identified and trained.

The Network Team needs to begin identifying and training people to do the consulting, present the Discovery sessions, write ministry position descriptions, and perform the other tasks necessary for successful Network implementation.

WHY IS IT IMPORTANT?

Phase 2 is important in order to prepare your church's Network Team, ministry leaders, and ministries for Phase 3, when Network "goes public."

CAUTION

If you skip this phase, people in your congregation who have gone through the Network Discovery sessions will become frustrated. The people who have completed the Network Discovery sessions will have an idea of where they should be serving, but the ministries will still try to "slot" them instead of placing them according to their *Servant Profiles*. The result will be confusion and resistance.

PHASE 2: MINISTRY PREPARATION

		2nd Discovery Seminar	Consultation		Network Pilot
Ministry Leaders Track A	**Identify Ministry Leaders** • People who will develop Network ministry position descriptions	**Ministry Leaders** • Personally experience Network • Attend the Discovery sessions	**Facilitate Consultations** • Senior leaders consult ministry leaders	**Develop Ministry Position Descriptions** • Ministry leaders develop ministry position descriptions • Identify and invite remaining leaders to attend Network Pilot	(Remaining Ministry Leaders attend Network Pilot)
Network Team Track B	**Identify Network Team Members** **Discovery Team** • Presenters • Small group leaders • Hosts and hostesses • Administrators **Consultation Team** • Consultants **Information Support Team** • Administrators • Data Processors	**Potential team members** • Personally experience Network • Attend the same Discovery Sessions as ministry leaders • Team leaders evaluate and modify Discovery sessions based on feedback as required	**Select and place Network Team members** • Network Team Leaders consult potential team members and commit to team	**Network Team prepares for full Network implementation (which includes the Network Pilot)** **Discovery Team** • Presenters • Hosts and hostesses determine logistics, etc. **Consultation Team** • Complete consultant training • Complete consultations within three weeks of Discovery Step **Information Support Team** • Prepare position descriptions and Ministry Booklet • Reproduce forms • Set-up database • Set-up tracking system • Prepare promotional strategy and material for Phase 3	**Network Team conducts Network Pilot** **Discovery Team** • Evaluates and modifies sessions based on feedback as appropriate **Consultation Team** • Consult **Information Support Team** • Data entry • Data Tracking (Determine if another pilot should be conducted)

HOW DO I GET THE MINISTRIES PREPARED?

This phase proceeds along two parallel tracks:

Track A: Integrate Ministry Leaders Into Network

Track B: Identify and Train Additional Network Team Leaders

Even though the following material presents ministry leader preparation first, keep in mind that these steps have to be conducted simultaneously.

TRACK A: INTEGRATE MINISTRY LEADERS INTO NETWORK

Why?

Here ministry leaders are asked to personally and organizationally commit to Network, and to develop ministry position descriptions for their ministry.

These ministry leaders are responsible for specific areas of ministry, and who report directly to senior leadership. They may be either paid or volunteer staff.

How?

STEP 1 **HAVE THE MINISTRY LEADERS PERSONALLY EXPERIENCE NETWORK**

The objective of this step is to get the ministry leaders to personally and organizationally commit to Network.

- It enhances a leader's ministry effectiveness.

- It enables the leader to more effectively serve volunteers being referred to his or her ministry.

- It creates commitment to develop ministry position descriptions.

- It increases understanding and support for Network.

1. Identify the people responsible for the different ministries and the people who will be responsible for developing the ministry position descriptions. These may or may not be the same people.

2. Invite those identified to experience the Network Discovery sessions. Have these persons RSVP, and set an alternate date for them to attend. Order materials.

3. Have them personally experience Network.

   • Take them through the Network Discovery sessions with their "leadership hats" off.

   • Encourage them to meet with their ministry leader for their "consultation."

   • Debrief and have them evaluate their Network experience.

4. Ask them if they will personally and organizationally commit to Network. Briefly inform them of the "next steps" including: consultation with senior leadership and developing ministry position descriptions.

5. Make necessary modifications based on feedback received.

STEP 2 **FACILITATE CONSULTATIONS BETWEEN SENIOR LEADERSHIP AND MINISTRY LEADERS**

The objective of this step is to honor your leaders and allow them to make any ministry adjustments that seem appropriate in light of their *Servant Profile*.

1. Encourage the consultations to occur within two weeks of the Network Discovery step. Send a note or memo to all involved to let them know by when the consultations should be completed.

2. Send a "thank you" for their participation and record "testimonials" for later reports and promotional materials. Be sure to get their approval to use these testimonials first.

STEP 3 **DEVELOP NETWORK MINISTRY POSITION DESCRIPTIONS**

The objective of this step is to compile a book of all the ministry positions available in the church, describing them in a uniform manner consistent with Network concepts (Passion, Spiritual Gifts, Personal Style, etc.). The Network Team uses these ministry descriptions to know each ministry's needs.

The Network Team member responsible for this activity should help the *ministry leaders* to develop these ministry position descriptions. By having the ministry leaders develop these descriptions, the descriptions will reflect the actual and future ministry needs as envisioned by the ministry leaders themselves. This way the ministry leaders will have *ownership* of the position descriptions, and their commitment to the Network approach to ministry will be strengthened.

The Network Team member responsible for this activity is responsible for editing the position descriptions to assure that they are consistent and for gathering information from ministry leaders who will not write position descriptions themselves.

1. Meet with ministry leaders who have attended the Network Discovery sessions.

   • Explain why ministry position descriptions are needed: Because this information is used by Network consultants to assist potential volunteers in understanding what serving possibilities are available to them in that ministry.

   • Explain how to complete a Ministry Position Description Form. A sample Ministry Position Description Form is found in the Appendix. You may copy or modify this form as needed for use in your Network ministry.

   • Inform the ministry leaders that as they develop these position descriptions they should not be limited to who they now have serving. They should prayerfully consider what kind of person they would like to have fulfill some area of ministry and then develop a position description. Descriptions should break the job down into manageable sizes. Some people may really be doing three positions, not one. If there is a need for a position to be filled twelve hours a week, have the ministry leader consider having three people serving in that position for four hours a week. The more options people have to serve, the greater the possibility of their serving.

   • Explain that they need to begin thinking about how volunteers will be:

   – Connected relationally to their ministry team.

   – Oriented to the ministry and its relationship to the church's vision.

   – Trained with the skills needed to fulfill the ministry position.

- Explain the "M" categories and encourage them to think "developmentally" so that they have positions in their ministry for all four categories. (See Appendix).

- Inform them of the date by which you need the ministry position descriptions returned.

- Invite them to contact you with any questions or concerns.

Some ministry leaders will immediately pick up on the idea and return well-defined descriptions. With some of your leaders, you will have to spend time helping them think through the positions in their ministry and developing proper descriptions.

Remember, the ministry leaders need to go through the Discovery sessions before they develop their ministry position descriptions. If not all of them were able to attend the first one, be sure that they attend the next one. You will then need to hold another meeting to explain how to complete the forms, or meet with each ministry leader individually to go through the information explained in this step.

2. Follow up with a phone call or meeting to determine if the ministry leaders have any questions or concerns. Determine those who will need you to sit with them and have you fill out the forms while asking them the questions. Set dates to meet with these people.

3. Compile and edit the ministry position descriptions. Be sure that they all use uniform language consistent with Network concepts. Edit those that sound like "commercials," or which seem boring. Keep in mind the following guidelines for writing the ministry position descriptions:

- Simplify the language as much as possible. For example, one ministry may call a position a "small group leader," while another ministry will use the title "facilitator" or "team coordinator." For the benefit of the volunteers and the consultants working with them, agree on what descriptive term will be used.

- Use the language of the ministry leaders who wrote the descriptions as much as possible, but remember it is important that the ministry position descriptions "read" as though they were written by one person. Create as much parity among the positions as possible. While some leaders are better communicators than others, you want to provide equal descriptions of excitement and opportunity.

- Do not force the Personal Style. Many positions really do not have a specific requirement. This is more of an art than a science. Imagine the best possible person to fill the position, then decide whether there is a preferred style, combination of styles, or no real style preference.

    - Keep the length and format of each description the same

4. Circulate the edited ministry position descriptions to the ministry leaders asking for their revisions or their OK. Set a required return date.

5. Revise the job descriptions and circulate them again for required signatures.

6. Compile final copies, duplicate, and put into notebooks for the consultants. Enter the information into the Network database.

7. Develop a ministries booklet. Many people are not aware of the church's different ministries. A Network Ministries Booklet provides the ministry name, a brief description, and a list of some ministry positions. Some sample Network Ministries Booklet entries for typical ministries are provided in the Appendix.

TRACK B: IDENTIFY AND TRAIN ADDITIONAL NETWORK TEAM MEMBERS

Why?

To develop a team to implement Network. Here new Network Team members are identified, recruited, and taken through the Network Discovery and Consultation steps.

How?

STEP 1 **IDENTIFY ADDITIONAL NETWORK TEAM MEMBERS**

The objective of this step is to identify people who can help implement Network:

1. Discovery Team

    - Discovery session presenters and/or small group leaders
    - Hosts and hostesses for registration, room set-up and take-down
    - Administrators to handle materials ordering, communications through the church bulletin and newsletter, etc.

2. Consultation Team

 • Consultants

3. Information Support Team

 • Administrators to handle editing and compiling the ministry position descriptions, creating the Network Ministry Booklet; duplicating the needed reporting forms (registration, consultation, *Personal Resources Survey*, etc.)

 • Data processors to handle: entering *Personal Resources Survey* and registration form data into the Network database; generating statistical reports about Network for tracking purposes.

Note: Keeping track of all the details connected with Network is a responsible job. This requires people who understand that each piece of information is not just impersonal data, but represents a person who matters to God and is committed to making their unique contribution through your church.

STEP 2 **HAVE POTENTIAL NETWORK TEAM MEMBERS PERSONALLY EXPERIENCE NETWORK**

The objective of this step is to obtain potential team members' personal commitment to Network, and to begin training them for their potential position.

1. Share the vision of Network with potential team members and invite them to experience it. Have them attend at the same time as the ministry leaders.

2. Inform them as to which aspects of Network to pay close attention. This experience also serves as training. Therefore, they need to know beforehand which aspects are particularly applicable to their potential Network position.

3. Assess who should be a part of the Network Team.

SELECT AND PLACE ADDITIONAL NETWORK TEAM MEMBERS

STEP 3

The objective of this step is to integrate new Network Team members into the Network Team.

1. Conduct consultations with potential team members. Have your current Network Team leaders conduct consultations with those who might report to them. Your current team

needs to feel comfortable with people with whom they will be working closely. Assess their commitment level, Passion, Spiritual Gifts, and skills for their potential position.

2. Invite those selected to be part of the Network Team. Discuss their job description and next steps to take.

3. Celebrate as a team! Take the opportunity to share the Network vision with them again.

STEP 4 **HAVE THE NEW NETWORK TEAM MEMBERS PREPARE FOR FULL NETWORK IMPLEMENTATION**

The objective of this step is to have the Network Team prepare for the Discovery pilot and implementation of Network.

1. Have the Discovery Team prepare for the Network Discovery Pilot.

   • Hosts and hostesses determine the logistics for the pilot and work with the Information Support Team on registration, etc.

   • Presenters prepare their material and determine who will be responsible for which sessions and parts of sessions (if you have more than one presenter).

   • Set a date to meet to evaluate the pilot after it is completed.

2. Have the Consultation Team prepare for the post-pilot consultations.

   • Consultants complete consultant training. See the Appendix for a suggested consultant training session, and refer to the Network Consultant's Guide for a complete discussion of conducting a Network consultation.

   • Determine how many consultations the consultants will be able to handle within three weeks of completing the pilot. Notify the Discovery Team and Information Support Team of this number to determine the maximum number of people the Network Pilot can accommodate. There is a sample Consultation Formula in the Appendix to help you with this.

3. Have the Information Support Team prepare for the Network Pilot, and for "going public" (Phase 3).

- Prepare Network Ministries Booklet (see the Appendix).

- Reproduce Network forms (registration, consulting, *Personal Resources Survey*, etc.).

- Set-up Network database.

- Set-up tracking system to follow Network participants from the Discovery Step through the Consultation Step into Service. A sample Tracking Form can be found in the Appendix.

- Prepare promotional material for *Phase 3: Network Implementation.* Consider flyers, posters, bulletin inserts, and announcements.

STEP 5 CONDUCT NETWORK DISCOVERY PILOT

The objective of this step is to conduct the Network Discovery pilot, which will serve as practice before going public in Phase 3.

1. The pilot should be attended by any senior leadership and ministry leaders who were unable to attend previous sessions, and by any "sub-ministry" leaders who have not yet completed the Network Discovery step.

2. Have the Discovery Team present the pilot, evaluate the presentation, and modify as required for future presentations.

3. Have the Consultation Team conduct consultations; identify areas of concern; evaluate consultants and provide constructive feedback; and modify as required for future consultations.

4. Have the Information Support Team enter the registration data and begin the tracking process, note any problems, evaluate and modify as required for the future.

5. Conduct another pilot, if necessary, to assure ample opportunity for all leaders to experience Network before "going public."

Are your ministries prepared?

Have you integrated your ministry leaders into Network?

Have you identified and trained additional Network Team Members?

Have

❑ The ministry leaders personally experienced Network?

❑ Senior leadership and ministry leaders experienced the Network Consultation?

❑ Network ministry position descriptions been developed?

❑ Potential Network Team Members been identified?

❑ Potential Network Team Members experienced Network?

❑ Additional Network Team Members been selected and placed in the Network Team?

❑ The new Network Team members prepared for full Network implementation?

Has

❑ The Network Discovery pilot been conducted?

Network Implementation

WHAT IS IT?

To cast the vision for Network to the congregation and begin guiding people to places of service according to their *Servant Profile*.

WHY IS IT IMPORTANT?

To demonstrate the value of Network to the congregation and enlist their commitment.

CAUTION

It is critical for the Network Team and senior leadership to clearly explain the personal and organizational benefits of Network to the congregation. Network should be presented as an opportunity, not a "have to."

PHASE 3: NETWORK IMPLEMENTATION

	Senior Leadership Communicates Vision To Congregation	Begin the Network Process			Conduct Network Team Meetings
		Discovery	Consultation	Service	
Senior Leadership and Ministry Leaders	• Sermon Series • Announcements, etc.			• Ministry contact between leaders and Network attendees	
Discovery Team and Consultation Team	• Register people for Network • Communicate future Network Discovery session dates	• Present sessions and obtain feedback • Evaluate and modify as necessary	• Consult within three weeks	• Follow-up calls to attendees • Record "success stories"	Entire Network Team: • Report and celebrate • Develop skills • Provide and encourage team building activities • Report to senior leadership and ministry leaders
Information Support Team		• Data entry • Tracking	• Data entry • Tracking	• Data entry • Tracking	• All of the above • Prepare reports for senior leader ship and ministry leaders

STEP 1 HAVE SENIOR LEADERSHIP COMMUNICATE ITS VISION FOR NETWORK TO THE CONGREGATION

Why?

To create interest, awareness, and excitement so they will want to personally experience Network.

How?

1. Have the Senior Pastor communicate the vision for Network from the pulpit. This can be done as part of a sermon series on serving. Other options include: announcements, testimonies, drama, and screening the Network Vision and Consultant Training video.

2. After the Senior Pastor communicates the vision for Network, introduce Network and how it will help your church function according to God's design for the church. Have promotional materials available. Provide easy access to registration for the Network Discovery sessions.

3. Register people for Network. Be sure to give them correct logistical information (length of program, time and number of sessions, location, cost, etc.).

4. Communicate future dates for Network Discovery sessions.

STEP 2 BEGIN THE NETWORK PROCESS

Why?

To have the congregation discover that they have a God-given Passion, Spiritual Gift, and Personal Style which impacts how they should serve.

How?

1. Conduct the Discovery sessions. Establish and communicate well in advance the dates, times, locations, and format of these sessions. Creatively offer them through the course of a year, so everyone will have had the opportunity to attend.

   • Present the sessions and obtain feedback

   • Evaluate and modify as necessary

   • Enter data (begin tracking)

2. Conduct consultations. The frequency and size of your Network sessions will depend on the number of consultants

you have. Participants should be consulted within two to three weeks after the completion of the session. Momentum is lost when it extends beyond three weeks. Pace yourselves. Using the Consultation Formula in the Appendix, calculate how many registrations you can take, given the number of consultants you have available.

- Evaluate and modify as necessary.

- Enter data (continue tracking).

3. Facilitate the service step.

- Notify ministry leaders of potential volunteers.
  - Make copies of the PRS form and send it to each leader of the ministries in which the volunteer expressed interest.
  - Notify the ministry leaders to contact volunteers within three days. It communicates to the volunteers your sincere interest in them.

- Make follow-up calls to those consulted to check on their progress, determine any problem areas, etc.

- Record "success stories."

STEP 3 CONDUCT NETWORK TEAM MEETINGS

Why?

To facilitate communication, skill development, and team unity.

How?

Schedule regular times when you can share stories, encourage one another, and rejoice. There is always new information that needs to be learned, and new insights that need to be shared.

1. Celebrate when groups of people complete all three Network Steps (Discovery, Consultation, and Service) by reporting on success stories and testimonials.

2. Train the Network Team in necessary skills.

3. Continue to provide and encourage team-building activities.

4. Provide feedback and report statistics to senior leadership and staff. Keeping records will prove to be valuable in spotting trends over time. Reporting is not just how many people attended, it is stories told of how lives are being impacted and changed for Christ. Count everything: books, money, refreshments, people, consultations, new volunteers, etc.

APPENDIX

The suggested training plan for becoming a Network consultant is:

1. Attend the Network Seminar
2. Be consulted
3. Observe two consultations *
4. Study ministry position descriptions
5. Review your church's structure of ministry and statement of faith
6. Training Day (Consultant's Guide) — a minimum of five hours is required.
7. Observe two consultations *
8. Join a consulting team with leader
9. Submit hours you are available to consult
10. BEGIN consulting

    * People in the *first* group of consultants in your church's Network ministry will not have the opportunity to observe consultations.

To conduct the training day

❑ Coordinate a date, time, and place for the training day

❑ Send a note to your consultants:
   - Thanking them for their participation
   - Detailing specifics of time, date, and place
   - Requesting that they complete the pre-class preparation in their Consultant's Guide. If they have not yet received a Consultant's Guide, be sure they receive one with the note.

❑ Follow-up with your consultants to confirm their attendance, and pre-class preparation

❑ Conduct the training day, using the Consultant's Guide as the outline for the training. The following is a guide to timing and sequence for the training day.

CONSULTANT TRAINING OUTLINE

Minimum Time Required (minutes)	Activity
	Note: You may need to adjust the time schedule to include breaks.
15	Welcome the participants and have them do the "Warming Up" activity found in the appendix of the Consultant's Guide.
70	Review the material in the Consultant's Guide.
60	Watch the Network Vision and Consultant Training Video and discuss.*
10	Introduce the Consulting Practice Exercise (Consultant's Guide appendix). Explain to the consultants the objectives of the exercise, and how to do it. Be sure that everyone understands the directions, and what they are supposed to do before you set them to doing it. Ask the consultants to get together in pairs. If there is an odd number of students, pair yourself with one of the consultants. Make sure the consultants know they have 45 minutes to complete each consultation and 15 minutes to organize and discuss how the person playing the consultant did.
60	Have the consultants start the exercise: After 40 minutes, let them know they have 5 minutes left for the consultation. After 45 minutes call time, and have them start the feedback and evaluation step. After 55 minutes, let them know they have 5 minutes left to complete the exercise.
10	After 60 minutes, call time and allow everyone to take a 10 minute break.
60	Reconvene the session, have the pairs switch, and the person who was the consultant become the volunteer, and vice versa.
15	Call the participants back together. Ask the group to share their insights on what they learned from the practice sessions. Use any remaining time to answer questions about Network in general or the Network implementation at your church.
300	**Total Time (5 hours)**

* You may want to stop the video at strategic points and
  discuss what was just seen.

CONSULTATION FORMULA

There is a general relationship between the number of people who register and attend Network Discovery sessions and those that actually get consulted. Here is a formula to get started. You will need to modify it as you get more experience.

Since you do not want more people coming to the Discovery sessions than you can consult in the following two to three weeks, you must start with how many consulting hours are available.

	Your Situation	Example
Consulting hours available in one week		
For example: 4 consultants available for 3 hours in one week = 12 hours plus one consultant available for 2 hours in one week = 2 hours equals a total of 14 consulting hours available per week)	_____	14
Times the weeks you will consult (2 or 3)	_____	X 3
Equals consulting hours per Discovery session	_____	= 42
Times 1.3 (this factor takes into account the attrition rate from the number of people who register to those who actually complete the consultation)	_____	X 1.3
Equals the amount of people you can register	_____	55

The difference is accounted for by people not being able to complete the Discovery sessions.

DISCOVERY SESSIONS CHECKLIST

Item	Who To Arrange:
1. Leader's Guide	
2. Participant's Guide	
3. Name tags, markers for writing names on the tags	
4. Overhead transparencies. Check before each class to be sure they are all there and in correct order.	
5. Overhead projector in proper working order, screen, extension cord, projection table, spare bulb, overhead projection markers.	
6. Network video cassette	
7. Video player and television set in proper working order, stand, extension cord, all necessary cables and connectors.	
8. Breaks, meals	

THE FOUR MINISTRY CATEGORIES

Faithfulness Factor	Ministry Category	Category Descriptions
Start Here	M1 ➡	• Minimum availability required: Limited • Gifts/Passion are untested • Skills/Experience not required • Minimum maturity required: Seeker • Church membership not required
Start Here	M2 ➡	• Minimum availability required: Limited • General Passion/Spiritual Gifts/Personal Style fit • Some skills/experience helpful • Minimum maturity required: New/Young Believer • Church membership not required
Developed Ministry Effectiveness With Relational Credibility	M3 ➡	• Minimum availability required: Moderate • Specific Passion/Spiritual Gifts/Personal Style fit • Specific skills/experience required • Minimum maturity required: Stable/growing believer • Church membership encouraged
Performing Major Ministry Responsibilities And Oversight	M4 ➡	• Minimum availability required: Significant • Proven Passion/Spiritual Gifts/Personal Style Affirmed • Proven skills/experience • Minimum maturity required: Leading/guiding believer • Church membership required • May require significant people management skills

Note: The "M" category is a description of where the volunteer is presently, not necessarily where the volunteer will be in the future.

GUIDELINES FOR DEVELOPING NEW MINISTRIES

Consider a basic four-step process to starting a ministry:

1. Identify the **Need**
2. Gather the **People**
3. Prepare the **Plan**
4. Affirm the **Leader**

The significance and timing of each of these is important.

STEP 1: IDENTIFY THE NEED

For a ministry to be considered, there must be a highly visible and identifiable need. This could be people to be served, or a problem to be solved. The need should be clearly felt and articulated. Ministries are not to be started just because other churches have one. Neither are they to continue just because they have always been done. A ministry must meet a need, but *a need does not necessitate a ministry!*

STEP 2: GATHER THE PEOPLE

When such a need has been identified, the next step is to form a group of those who are interested, appropriately gifted, and exhibit a genuine Passion to see that need met. They meet for prayer and discussion. Through wisdom and time these people formulate a clear vision for the ministry.

STEP 3: PREPARE THE PLAN

When consensus has been achieved on the need and a vision to meet that need, it is time to develop a ministry plan. Continue to meet together until the details and strategy of a ministry plan are worked through. This can typically require twelve- to twenty-four months. After a plan is presented and approved, there is still one very important step: Affirm the Leader.

STEP 4: AFFIRM THE LEADER

Before you put a plan in motion, the leader needs to be affirmed. Even though the need, the people, and the program are in place, without the *right* leader, a ministry should not be started. Affirmed leadership will take appropriate responsibility for the ministry. Without the right leader, problems may be quickly given to the staff for resolution. As a staff person, "Do *you* want to lead this ministry?" If not, then wait for the Head of the church to identify such a person.

Ministries are best started when there is a clear need, gifted people, a strategic plan, and an affirmed leader.

MINISTRY POSITION DESCRIPTION

POSITION TITLE	MINISTRY	DEPARTMENT	M-LEVEL
BIG BUDDY	BUDDY	ELEMENTARY	3

Responsibilities

To be a Christian role model and develop relationships with children from single-parent homes.

Passion for

Mentoring and discipling the young who have lost a parent through death or divorce.

Spiritual Gifts

Shepherding
Mercy
Encouragement

Personal Style

Energized   ☒ People-Oriented
        ❏ Task-Oriented

Organized   ☒ Structured
        ☒ Unstructured

Minimum Spiritual maturity

Stable/Growing

Talents/Skill/Abilities

Communicate well with children. Plan creative activities, sports, crafts, etc.

Availability

☒ Flexible

Mon	Tues	Wed	Thur	Fri	Sat	Sun

Regular Commitments

Bi-monthly Thursday meetings before church (6 per yr)

Length of Commitment

1 year

ADDITIONAL COMMENTS

Minimum for 2-4 hours weekly.
Paired with same-sex child

LOCATION

❏ Church   ☒ Home   ❏ Other:

SPECIAL NOTES

Membership Encouraged

Total Needed | 8   Now Have | 5   Openings | 3

Staff Overseer _____

Trained By _____

Assimilator _____

Date Modified
12/16/93

DateCreated
12/8/93

MINISTRY POSITION DESCRIPTION

POSITION TITLE	MINISTRY	DEPARTMENT	M-LEVEL
DAYTIME ASSISTANT	BUILDING SERVICES	BUILDING SERVICES	1

Responsibilities

Runs errands for various ministries. Assists Building Services staff with various tasks.

Passion for

Maintaining a quality facility, so that whoever enters our building may grow in their understanding of Christ in an environment free of distractions.

Spiritual Gifts

Helps

Personal Style

Energized   ❏ People-Oriented
           ☒ Task-Oriented

Organized   ❏ Structured
           ☒ Unstructured

Minimum Spiritual maturity

Seeker

Talents/Skill/Abilities

Must be able to drive.

Availability   ☒ Flexible

Mon	Tues	Wed	Thur	Fri	Sat	Sun

Regular Commitments

Length of Commitment

ADDITIONAL COMMENTS

Needs to be a "whatever it takes" kind of person. Whatever is needed at the time is what these people will do.

LOCATION

☒ Church   ❏ Home   ❏ Other:

SPECIAL NOTES

Total Needed | 3   Now Have | 1   Openings | 2

Staff Overseer _____

Trained By _____

Assimilator _____

Date Modified
12/16/93

DateCreated
12/8/93

MINISTRY POSITION DESCRIPTION

POSITION TITLE	MINISTRY	DEPARTMENT	M-LEVEL
MAINTENANCE TEAM MEMBER	BUILDING SERVICES	BUILDING SERVICES	1

Responsibilities

Helps team do an assortment of janitorial and building maintenance projects.

Passion for

Maintaining a quality facility, so that whoever enters our building may grow in their understanding of Christ in an environment free of distractions.

Spiritual Gifts

Helps
Craftsmanship

Personal Style

Energized ☐ People-Oriented
☒ Task-Oriented

Organized ☒ Structured
☐ Unstructured

Minimum Spiritual maturity

Seeker

Talents/Skill/Abilities

Professional trades or handyman skills
Training people
Dependable/Accountable

Availability

☒ Flexible

Mon	Tues	Wed	Thur	Fri	Sat	Sun
R	R					

Regular Commitments

Mondays 6:30-9:00p.m. or Tuesday 6:30-9:00p.m.

Length of Commitment

1 year

ADDITIONAL COMMENTS

LOCATION

☒ Church   ☐ Home   ☐ Other:

SPECIAL NOTES

Total Needed 4   Now Have 5   Openings -1

Staff Overseer _____

Trained By _____

Assimilator _____

Date Modified
12/16/93

DateCreated
12/8/93

MINISTRY POSITION DESCRIPTION

POSITION TITLE	MINISTRY	DEPARTMENT	M-LEVEL
CAREER CONSULTANT	CAREERS	ADULT MINISTRIES	4

Responsibilities

Motivates and assists career planning and job search.

Passion for

Assisting individuals in realizing their full potential for meaningful and gainful employment through a biblical understanding of work.

Spiritual Gifts

Wisdom
Encouragement
Discernment

Personal Style

Energized ☒ People-Oriented
❏ Task-Oriented

Organized ☒ Structured
☒ Unstructured

Minimum Spiritual maturity

Stable/Growing

Talents/Skill/Abilities

Good listener
Good confronter/challenger
Good interviewer

Availability   ☒ Flexible

Mon	Tues	Wed	Thur	Fri	Sat	Sun
R						

Regular Commitments

Monday p.m.

Length of Commitment

1 year

ADDITIONAL COMMENTS

LOCATION

☒ Church   ❏ Home   ❏ Other:

SPECIAL NOTES

Membership Encouraged

Total Needed 2   *Now Have* 1   *Openings* 1

MINISTRY POSITION DESCRIPTION

POSITION TITLE	MINISTRY	DEPARTMENT	M-LEVEL
DEFENDERS REFERRAL TEAM	DEFENDERS	EVANGELISM	3

Responsibilities

Use expertise in the area of apologetics, to provide answers to the intellectual questions hindering seekers from trusting Christ.

Passion for

Presenting Christianity in a positive, compelling, and humble manner.

Spiritual Gifts

Evangelism
Knowledge
Discernment
Teaching/Wisdom

Personal Style

Energized ☒ People-Oriented
         ❏ Task-Oriented

Organized ❏ Structured
         ☒ Unstructured

Minimum Spiritual maturity

Stable/Growing

Talents/Skill/Abilities

Availability

☒ Flexible

Mon	Tues	Wed	Thur	Fri	Sat	Sun

Regular Commitments

Meeting once a month

Length of Commitment

1 year

ADDITIONAL COMMENTS

LOCATION

☒ Church   ☒ Home   ☒ Other:

SPECIAL NOTES

Membership Encouraged

Total Needed   *Now Have*   *Openings*

Staff Overseer _____

Trained By _____

Assimilator _____

Date Modified
12/16/93

DateCreated
12/8/93

MINISTRY POSITION DESCRIPTION

POSITION TITLE	MINISTRY	DEPARTMENT	M-LEVEL
DRAMA TEAM MEMBER	DRAMA	PROGRAMMING	2

Responsibilities

Acts in drama sketches.
Attends a mandatory class weekly.

Passion for

Presenting real-life, contemporary drama sketches designed to heighten awareness to the speaker's topic.

Spiritual Gifts

Creative Communication
Encouragement

Personal Style

Energized ☒ People-Oriented
☒ Task-Oriented

Organized ☒ Structured
❏ Unstructured

Minimum Spiritual maturity

New/Young

Talents/Skill/Abilities

Experience or extreme interest in acting

Availability

☒ Flexible

Mon	Tues	Wed	Thur	Fri	Sat	Sun

Regular Commitments

Rehearsals 7:00-8:30p.m. Tuesday

Length of Commitment

1 year

ADDITIONAL COMMENTS

Rehersals take place on Thursday nights and Saturday afternoons for those involved in that week's drama. Everyone is to attend each training session on Tuesday evenings.

LOCATION

☒ Church ❏ Home ❏ Other:

SPECIAL NOTES

Must Audition

Total Needed   *Now Have*   *Openings*

Staff Overseer _____

Trained By _____

Assimilator _____

Date Modified
12/16/93

DateCreated
12/8/93

MINISTRY POSITION DESCRIPTION

POSITION TITLE	MINISTRY	DEPARTMENT	M-LEVEL
WRITER	DRAMA	PROGRAMMING	3

Responsibilities

Writes 5-8 minute dramatic sketches around a topic for weekend and special services, from a topic assigned in advance.

Sketches need to have high audience identification and be able to engage audience's emotions.

Passion for

Presenting real-life, contemporary drama sketches designed to heighten awareness to the speaker's topic.

Spiritual Gifts

Creative Communication
Teaching
Prophecy

Personal Style

Energized
☐ People-Oriented
☒ Task-Oriented

Organized
☒ Structured
☐ Unstructured

Minimum Spiritual maturity

New/Young

Talents/Skill/Abilities

Must have experience in creative writing, drama, sit-coms

Availability

☒ Flexible

Mon	Tues	Wed	Thur	Fri	Sat	Sun

Regular Commitments

monthly meeting

Length of Commitment

6 months

ADDITIONAL COMMENTS

LOCATION

☐ Church   ☒ Home   ☐ Other:

SPECIAL NOTES

Total Needed [4]   Now Have [2]   Openings [2]

Staff Overseer _____

Trained By _____

Assimilator _____

Date Modified
12/16/93

DateCreated
12/8/93

MINISTRY POSITION DESCRIPTION

POSITION TITLE	MINISTRY	DEPARTMENT	M-LEVEL
BUDGET COUNSELOR	GOOD SENSE	PASTORAL CARE	3

Responsibilities

One on one counseling on financial, budget and money control.

Passion for

Discipling people in the principle of biblical stewardship.

Spiritual Gifts

Encouragement
Discernment
Wisdom
Administration

Personal Style

Energized ☒ People-Oriented
☒ Task-Oriented

Organized ☒ Structured
❑ Unstructured

Minimum Spiritual maturity

Stable/Growing

Talents/Skill/Abilities

Relational skills
Accountable for own finances
Living on and within a budget

Availability

☒ Flexible

Mon	Tues	Wed	Thur	Fri	Sat	Sun

Regular Commitments

Quarterly team meetings
Ocassional training events/meeting

Length of Commitment

1 year

ADDITIONAL COMMENTS

LOCATION

☒ Church   ❑ Home   ☒ Other:

SPECIAL NOTES

Membership Required

Total Needed | 8   Now Have | 5   Openings | 3

Staff Overseer _____

Trained By _____

Assimilator _____

Date Modified
12/16/93

DateCreated
12/8/93

MINISTRY POSITION DESCRIPTION

POSITION TITLE	MINISTRY	DEPARTMENT	M-LEVEL
ADOPT A BED	GROUNDS	GROUNDS	1

Responsibilities

Tends and cares for specific flower beds or groups of trees by weeding, cultivating, and flower picking.

Passion for

Creating and maintaining environment which reflects God excellence in nature.

Spiritual Gifts

Helps

Personal Style

Energized ☐ People-Oriented
☒ Task-Oriented

Organized ☐ Structured
☒ Unstructured

Minimum Spiritual maturity

Seeker

Talents/Skill/Abilities

Working with hands
Enjoys working outdoors with plants

Availability ☒ Flexible

Mon	Tues	Wed	Thur	Fri	Sat	Sun

Regular Commitments

Monthly team meeting

Length of Commitment

1 year

ADDITIONAL COMMENTS
Knowledge of flowers helpful

LOCATION

☐ Church   ☐ Home   ☐ Other:

SPECIAL NOTES

Total Needed 7   Now Have 5   Openings 2

Staff Overseer _____

Trained By _____

Assimilator _____

Date Modified
12/16/93

DateCreated
12/8/93

MINISTRY POSITION DESCRIPTION

POSITION TITLE	MINISTRY	DEPARTMENT	M-LEVEL
NURSING HOME VISITATION	HERITAGE	PASTORAL CARE	2

Responsibilities

To visit one or more lonely and forgotten nursing home residents on a regular basis with the objective of building a relationship with them. Ministering spiritually, emotionally, and practically.

Passion for

Caring for people by providing quality care and spiritual support that values the individual while attending to their aging needs.

Spiritual Gifts

Mercy
Encouragement

Personal Style

Energized ☒ People-Oriented
❑ Task-Oriented

Organized ☒ Structured
❑ Unstructured

Minimum Spiritual maturity

Stable/Growing

Talents/Skill/Abilities

The ability to be a good friend & listener and to share God's love and word

Availability

☒ Flexible

Mon	Tues	Wed	Thur	Fri	Sat	Sun
0			0			
0			0			
0			0			

Regular Commitments

Length of Commitment

1 year

ADDITIONAL COMMENTS

LOCATION

❑ Church   ❑ Home   ☒ Other:

SPECIAL NOTES

Membership Encouraged

Total Needed 8   Now Have 4   Openings 4

Staff Overseer _____

Trained By _____

Assimilator _____

Date Modified
12/16/93

DateCreated
12/8/93

MINISTRY POSITION DESCRIPTION

POSITION TITLE	MINISTRY	DEPARTMENT	M-LEVEL
COMPUTER SERVICE COORDINATOR	INFORMATION SYSTEM	COMPUTER	4

Responsibilities

Interviews volunteers to determine compatibility, delegate responsibilities, and schedule work load.

Passion for

Providing the ministries of the church information systems and support that enable those ministries to serve with more efficiency and effectiveness.

Spiritual Gifts

Discernment
Shepherding
Helps

Personal Style

Energized ☒ People-Oriented
☒ Task-Oriented

Organized ☒ Structured
☐ Unstructured

Minimum Spiritual maturity

Leading/Guiding

Talents/Skill/Abilities

Professional experience required

Availability

☒ Flexible

Mon	Tues	Wed	Thur	Fri	Sat	Sun

Regular Commitments

Flexible

Length of Commitment

1 year

ADDITIONAL COMMENTS

LOCATION

☒ Church   ☐ Home   ☐ Other:

SPECIAL NOTES

Membership Encouraged

Total Needed 1   *Now Have* 1   *Openings* 1

Staff Overseer _____

Trained By _____

Assimilator _____

Date Modified
12/16/93

DateCreated
12/8/93

MINISTRY POSITION DESCRIPTION

POSITION TITLE	MINISTRY	DEPARTMENT	M-LEVEL
WEDDING CONSULTANT	MARRIAGE	ADULT MINISTRIES	2

Responsibilities

Work with engaged couples to plan their wedding.

Coordinate wedding ceremonies and rehearsals.

Passion for

Assisting couples to build God-honoring marriages.

Spiritual Gifts

Hospitality
Encouragement
Discernment

Personal Style

Energized ☒ People-Oriented
☒ Task-Oriented

Organized ☒ Structured
❏ Unstructured

Minimum Spiritual maturity

New/Young

Talents/Skill/Abilities

Confident in dealing with people

Availability

☒ Flexible

Mon	Tues	Wed	Thur	Fri	Sat	Sun

Regular Commitments

Flexible

Length of Commitment

1 year

ADDITIONAL COMMENTS

LOCATION

☒ Church   ❏ Home   ❏ Other:

SPECIAL NOTES

Total Needed | 3   Now Have | 2   Openings | 1

Staff Overseer _____

Trained By _____

Assimilator _____

Date Modified
12/16/93

DateCreated
12/8/93

MINISTRY POSITION DESCRIPTION

POSITION TITLE	MINISTRY	DEPARTMENT	M-LEVEL
ADMINISTRATOR (SEMINAR/SM GRPS)	NETWORK	NETWORK	2

Responsibilities

Responsible for all the details associated with Network's Discovery sessions, including publicity, announcements, expenses, ordering manuals, registration, check-in, and keeping accurate records for the Information Support Team.

Passion for

Assisting believers to make their unique contribution in a meaningful place of service.

Designing and developing excellent systems to serve people better.

Spiritual Gifts

Administration
Helps
Wisdom
Creative Communication

Personal Style

Energized	❏ People-Oriented
	☒ Task-Oriented
Organized	☒ Structured
	❏ Unstructured

Minimum Spiritual maturity

New/Young

Talents/Skill/Abilities

Detail-oriented, resourceful
Able to manage multiple issues
Communicates well

Availability   ☒ Flexible

Mon	Tues	Wed	Thur	Fri	Sat	Sun

Regular Commitments

Monthly team meetings

Length of Commitment

1 year

ADDITIONAL COMMENTS

1-2 hrs/wk needed when there are not sessions being done.
3-4 hrs/wk needed during those weeks when there are Discovery sessions being done.

LOCATION

☒ Church   ❏ Home   ❏ Other:

SPECIAL NOTES

Total Needed | 2   Now Have | 1   Openings | 1

Staff Overseer _____

Trained By _____

Assimilator _____

Date Modified
12/16/93

DateCreated
12/8/93

MINISTRY POSITION DESCRIPTION

POSITION TITLE	MINISTRY	DEPARTMENT	M-LEVEL
INFO SUPPORT TEAM MEMBER	NETWORK	NETWORK	2

Responsibilities

Responsible for gathering and processing information needed for consultants, the Network ministry and the church including: registrations, attendance lists, consultation schedules, follow-up reports, etc.

Passion for

Assisting believers to make their unique contribution in a meaningful place of service.

Information and systems that serve people, and help the church to be more effective and efficient.

Spiritual Gifts

Administration
Helps
Craftsmanship

Personal Style

Energized   ❏ People-Oriented
  ☒ Task-Oriented

Organized   ☒ Structured
  ❏ Unstructured

Minimum Spiritual maturity

New/Young

Talents/Skill/Abilities

Project management abilities
Dependable
Able to do data entry
Basic computer skills

Availability   ☒ Flexible

Mon	Tues	Wed	Thur	Fri	Sat	Sun

Regular Commitments

Scheduled team meetings
2-3 hrs/wk

Length of Commitment

1 year

ADDITIONAL COMMENTS

LOCATION

☒ Church   ❏ Home   ❏ Other:

SPECIAL NOTES

Total Needed | 4   Now Have | 2   Openings | 2

Staff Overseer _____

Trained By _____

Assimilator _____

Date Modified
12/16/93

DateCreated
12/8/93

MINISTRY POSITION DESCRIPTION

POSITION TITLE	MINISTRY	DEPARTMENT	M-LEVEL
CONSULTANT	NETWORK	NETWORK	3

Responsibilities

Responsible to assist Network participants one-on-one in identifying possible and appropriate places of service. Needs to listen, discern, and serve the individual. Needs to interpret the Servant Profile and identify ministry opportunities for the volunteer.

Passion for

Assisting believers to make their unique contribution in a meaningful place of service.

Helping people become all they can be in Christ.

Spiritual Gifts

Wisdom
Discernment
Encouragement
Knowledge

Personal Style

Energized ☒ People-Oriented
           ❏ Task-Oriented

Organized ☒ Structured
           ☒ Unstructured

Minimum Spiritual maturity

Stable/Growing

Talents/Skill/Abilities

Counseling skills, listens well
Good with first impressions
Able to speak the truth in love

Availability   ☒ Flexible

Mon	Tues	Wed	Thur	Fri	Sat	Sun

Regular Commitments

Team Meetings, Consultant training events, 3-4 hrs/wk

Length of Commitment

1 year

ADDITIONAL COMMENTS

Consultants need to be caring and respected people. They need to be familiar with the church, its history and philosophy.

LOCATION

☒ Church   ❏ Home   ❏ Other:

SPECIAL NOTES

Membership Encouraged

Total Neede	Now Have	Openings
12	9	3

Staff Overseer _____

Trained By   _____

Assimilator   _____

Date Modified
12/16/93

DateCreated
12/8/93

MINISTRY POSITION DESCRIPTION

POSITION TITLE	MINISTRY	DEPARTMENT	M-LEVEL
FOLLOW-UP COORDINATOR	NETWORK	NETWORK	3

Responsibilities

Responsible to follow-up on participants all the way through the Network process, from the registration for the Discovery sessions to Serving; encouraging them and assisting them on how they can reach their place of ministry.

Passion for

Assisting believers to make their unique contribution in a meaningful place of service.

People to know their value and worth to God and the church.

Spiritual Gifts

Encouragement
Hospitality
Administration

Personal Style

Energized   ☒ People-Oriented
          ❑ Task-Oriented

Organized   ☒ Structured
          ❑ Unstructured

Minimum Spiritual maturity

Stable/Growing

Talents/Skill/Abilities

Able to make people feel valued
Positive attitude, does not offend
Excellent phone skills, pleasant voice

Availability

☒ Flexible

Mon	Tues	Wed	Thur	Fri	Sat	Sun

Regular Commitments

Team meetings as scheduled
1-2 hrs/wk depending on size of sessions

Length of Commitment

1 year

ADDITIONAL COMMENTS

LOCATION

❑ Church   ☒ Home   ❑ Other:

SPECIAL NOTES

Membership Encouraged

Total Needed | 1   Now Have | 0   Openings | 1

Staff Overseer _____

Trained By _____

Assimilator _____

Date Modified
12/16/93

DateCreated
12/8/93

MINISTRY POSITION DESCRIPTION

POSITION TITLE	MINISTRY	DEPARTMENT	M-LEVEL
HOSPITALITY COORDINATOR	NETWORK	NETWORK	3

Responsibilities

Responsible for creating a quality atmosphere for participants to learn and grow. This includes the coordination of the room set-up, refreshments, assisting the instructor, greeting participants, and assuring that everyone's needs are met for the sessions.

Passion for

Assisting believers to make their unique contribution in a meaningful place of service.

Assimilating people into the life and ministry of the church.

Spiritual Gifts

Hospitality
Encouragement
Helps
Creative Communication

Personal Style

Energized ☒ People-Oriented
           ❏ Task-Oriented

Organized ☒ Structured
           ☒ Unstructured

Minimum Spiritual maturity

Stable/Growing

Talents/Skill/Abilities

Able to anticipate needs and meet them
Has warm personality
Creative and fun

Availability   ☒ Flexible

Mon	Tues	Wed	Thur	Fri	Sat	Sun

Regular Commitments

Monthly team meeting and others as scheduled

Length of Commitment

1 year

ADDITIONAL COMMENTS
3-4 hrs/wk during Discovery sessions

LOCATION

☒ Church   ❏ Home   ❏ Other:

SPECIAL NOTES

Membership Encouraged

Total Needed | 1   Now Have | 0   Openings | 1

Staff Overseer _____

Trained By _____

Assimilator _____

Date Modified
12/16/93

DateCreated
12/8/93

MINISTRY POSITION DESCRIPTION

POSITION TITLE	MINISTRY	DEPARTMENT	M-LEVEL
CONSULTANT TRAINER	NETWORK	NETWORK	4

Responsibilities

Responsible to train new consultants in the necessary skills and ministry concepts to conduct effective consultations, also providing on-going training opportunities as needed.

Passion for

Assisting believers to make their unique contribution in a meaningful place of service.

Teaching vital skills and ministry concepts to those who want to be more effective in serving others.

Spiritual Gifts

Wisdom
Discernment
Teaching
Knowledge

Personal Style

Energized   ☒ People-Oriented
             ☒ Task-Oriented

Organized   ☒ Structured
             ❑ Unstructured

Minimum Spiritual maturity

Stable/Growing

Talents/Skill/Abilities

Counseling skills
Able to train and develop
Good presentation skills

Availability   ☒ Flexible

Mon	Tues	Wed	Thur	Fri	Sat	Sun

Regular Commitments

Provide training as needed, meetings as scheduled

Length of Commitment

2 years

ADDITIONAL COMMENTS

15-18 hrs are required for preparation to do the 6-8 hrs of new consultant training (it will decrease with experience). On-going training and preparation will vary depending upon the topic, quest speaker, etc.

LOCATION

☒ Church   ❑ Home   ❑ Other:

SPECIAL NOTES

Membership Encouraged

Total Needed | 1   Now Have | 1   Openings | 0

Staff Overseer _____

Trained By _____

Assimilator _____

Date Modified
12/16/93

DateCreated
12/8/93

MINISTRY POSITION DESCRIPTION

POSITION TITLE	MINISTRY	DEPARTMENT	M-LEVEL
CONSULTATION COORDINATOR	NETWORK	NETWORK	4

Responsibilities

Responsible for all aspects of the consultation step: recruiting, training and overseeing a team of consultants, maintaining follow-up, insuring updated information and ministry descriptions

Passion for

Assisting believers to make their unique contribution in a meaningful place of service.

Seeing people develop into their full potential in Christ.

Spiritual Gifts

Discernment
Wisdom
Leadership
Encouragement

Personal Style

Energized   ☒ People-Oriented
           ❏ Task-Oriented

Organized   ☒ Structured
           ☒ Unstructured

Minimum Spiritual maturity

Leading/Guiding

Talents/Skill/Abilities

Counseling skills, listens well
Good with first impressions
Team builder, able to train and develop

Availability

☒ Flexible

Mon	Tues	Wed	Thur	Fri	Sat	Sun

Regular Commitments

Monthly Team meetings, one-on-one meetings as required, 6-10 hrs/wk

Length of Commitment

2+ years

ADDITIONAL COMMENTS

This person needs to be very good at speaking the truth in love. They also need to be able to develop and coach those who will be consulting. Their goal ought to be to serve the volunteer in identifying and moving toward the fulfillment of their ministry.

LOCATION

☒ Church   ❏ Home   ❏ Other:

SPECIAL NOTES

Membership Required

Total Needed | 1   Now Have | 1   Openings | 0

Staff Overseer _____

Trained By _____

Assimilator _____

Date Modified
12/16/93

DateCreated
12/8/93

MINISTRY POSITION DESCRIPTION

POSITION TITLE	MINISTRY	DEPARTMENT	M-LEVEL
DISCOVERY SESSION COORDINATOR	NETWORK	NETWORK	4

Responsibilities

Responsible for all aspects of conducting the seminar and/or small groups going through Network's Discovery sessions, recruiting and building a team to lead and support the seminar/small groups, identify instructors.

Passion for

Assisting believers to make their unique contribution in a meaningful place of service by presenting God's truths with excellence.

Seeing people develop into their full potential in Christ.

Spiritual Gifts

Leadership
Encouragement
Teaching
Hospitality

Personal Style

Energized ☒ People-Oriented
❏ Task-Oriented

Organized ☒ Structured
❏ Unstructured

Minimum Spiritual maturity

Leading/Guiding

Talents/Skill/Abilities

Good interpersonal skill
Able to recruit and delagate
Organizational

Availability   ☒ Flexible

Mon	Tues	Wed	Thur	Fri	Sat	Sun

Regular Commitments

Monthly Team meetings, one-on-one meetings as required, 6-10 hrs/wk

Length of Commitment

2+ years

ADDITIONAL COMMENTS

LOCATION

☒ Church   ❏ Home   ❏ Other:

SPECIAL NOTES

Membership Required

Total Needed | 1   *Now Have* | 1   *Openings* | 0

Staff Overseer _____

Trained By _____

Assimilator _____

Date Modified
12/16/93

DateCreated
12/8/93

MINISTRY POSITION DESCRIPTION

POSITION TITLE	MINISTRY	DEPARTMENT	M-LEVEL
INFORMATION SUPPORT COORDINATOR	NETWORK	NETWORK	4

Responsibilities

Responsible for all data systems and information flow within Network, keeping sub-ministry job descriptions updated, scheduling facilities and resources.

Passion for

Assisting believers to make their unique contribution in a meaningful place of service.

The Church to maximize its resources for the Kingdom.

Spiritual Gifts

Administration
Helps
Leadership

Personal Style

Energized ❏ People-Oriented
         ☒ Task-Oriented

Organized ☒ Structured
         ❏ Unstructured

Minimum Spiritual maturity

Leading/Guiding

Talents/Skill/Abilities

Strategic thinker, organized
Able to manage projects and flow
Team builder

Availability

☒ Flexible

Mon	Tues	Wed	Thur	Fri	Sat	Sun

Regular Commitments

Monthly Team meetings, one-on-one meetings as required, 6-10 hrs/wk

Length of Commitment

2+ years

ADDITIONAL COMMENTS

A knowledge of computers is helpful. They need to keep all the pieces of Network together within a timely and good communication system

LOCATION

☒ Church   ❏ Home   ❏ Other:

SPECIAL NOTES

Membership Encouraged

Total Needed 1   Now Have 1   Openings 0

Staff Overseer _____

Trained By _____

Assimilator _____

Date Modified
12/16/93

DateCreated
12/8/93

MINISTRY POSITION DESCRIPTION

POSITION TITLE	MINISTRY	DEPARTMENT	M-LEVEL
INSTRUCTOR	NETWORK	NETWORK	4

Responsibilities

Responsible for preparing and presenting Network's eight Discovery sessions.

Passion for

Assisting believers to make their unique contribution in a meaningful place of service.

Assisting believers to better understand who God has made them to be for greater fruitfulness and fulfillment in their ministry.

Spiritual Gifts

Encouragement
Teaching
Wisdom

Personal Style

Energized ☒ People-Oriented
☒ Task-Oriented

Organized ☒ Structured
❑ Unstructured

Minimum Spiritual maturity

Leading/Guiding

Talents/Skill/Abilities

High capacity to integrate
Effective communicator
Excellent interpersonal skills

Availability

☒ Flexible

Mon	Tues	Wed	Thur	Fri	Sat	Sun
						O
O	O		O			

Regular Commitments

Monthly team meeting, feedback and evaluation time

Length of Commitment

1 year

ADDITIONAL COMMENTS

There is flexible study and preparation time. When the sessions are scheduled, then the availability chart can be completed above. There is preparation time of 3-4 hrs/wk when leading the sessions and 8 hrs of presentation time.

LOCATION

☒ Church   ❑ Home   ❑ Other:

SPECIAL NOTES

Membership Encouraged

Total Needed | 2   Now Have | 1   Openings | 1

Staff Overseer _____

Trained By _____

Assimilator _____

Date Modified
12/16/93

DateCreated
12/8/93

MINISTRY POSITION DESCRIPTION

POSITION TITLE	MINISTRY	DEPARTMENT	M-LEVEL
NETWORK DIRECTOR	NETWORK	NETWORK	4

Responsibilities

Responsible for casting the Network vision, overseeing the team, mediating between staff, ministry leaders and volunteers, representing Network to each of these groups, promoting the values and opportunities for service.

Passion for

Assisting believers to make their unique contribution in a meaningful place of service.

The church and seeing people develop into their full potential in Christ.

Spiritual Gifts

Leadership
Wisdom
Encouragement
Administration

Personal Style

Energized ☒ People-Oriented
☒ Task-Oriented

Organized ☒ Structured
❑ Unstructured

Minimum Spiritual maturity

Leading/Guiding

Talents/Skill/Abilities

Good interpersonal skill
Organizational, effective delegator
Sensitive, listens well

Availability   ☒ Flexible

Mon	Tues	Wed	Thur	Fri	Sat	Sun

Regular Commitments

Monthly Team meetings, one-on-one meetings as required, 6-10 hrs/wk

Length of Commitment

2+ years

ADDITIONAL COMMENTS

Must be highly respected by both staff and volunteers
Professional background helpful, but not required

LOCATION

☒ Church   ☒ Home   ❑ Other:

SPECIAL NOTES

Membership Required

Total Needed | 1   Now Have | 1   Openings | 1

Staff Overseer _____

Trained By _____

Assimilator _____

Date Modified
12/16/93

DateCreated
12/8/93

MINISTRY POSITION DESCRIPTION

POSITION TITLE	MINISTRY	DEPARTMENT	M-LEVEL
SUMMER STAFF ASSISTANT	PROMISELAND	CHILDREN'S DEPT	1

Responsibilities

Small group leaders (will stagger time with permanent leaders) to support the Promiseland teaching team by supervising small groups of children.

Passion for

Helping children understand who God is, so that in God's timing, the child will come to have a personal relationship with Jesus Christ.

Spiritual Gifts

Helps
Teaching
Administration
Shepherding

Personal Style

Energized   ☒ People-Oriented
          ❏ Task-Oriented

Organized   ❏ Structured
          ☒ Unstructured

Minimum Spiritual maturity

Seeker

Talents/Skill/Abilities

Likes and enjoys children

Availability   ☒ Flexible

Mon	Tues	Wed	Thur	Fri	Sat	Sun
						R
					R	

Regular Commitments

Length of Commitment

4-11 weeks

ADDITIONAL COMMENTS

LOCATION

☒ Church   ❏ Home   ❏ Other:

SPECIAL NOTES

Total Needed 28   *Now Have* 16   *Openings* 12

Staff Overseer _____

Trained By _____

Assimilator _____

Date Modified
12/16/93

DateCreated
12/8/93

MINISTRY POSITION DESCRIPTION

POSITION TITLE	MINISTRY	DEPARTMENT	M-LEVEL
GROUP FACILITATOR	REBUILDERS	ADULT MINISTRIES	3

Responsibilities

Facilitate small discussion groups for individuals experiencing relationship loss due to failing or failed marriage.

Passion for

Providing biblical insights and relational support to anyone who has experienced marital breakdown, separation or divorce in order to bring them to a resolution that honors God.

Spiritual Gifts

Encouragement
Counseling
Shepherding
Wisdom

Personal Style

Energized ☒ People-Oriented
☐ Task-Oriented

Organized ☒ Structured
☐ Unstructured

Minimum Spiritual maturity

Stable/Growing

Talents/Skill/Abilities

Lead group discussion

Availability   ☐ Flexible

Mon	Tues	Wed	Thur	Fri	Sat	Sun
R						

Regular Commitments

Mondays 6:30-9:30 pm meeting once/month for leaders

Length of Commitment

6 months

ADDITIONAL COMMENTS

LOCATION

☐ Church   ☐ Home   ☐ Other:

SPECIAL NOTES

Membership Encouraged

Total Needed 5   Now Have 4   Openings 1

Staff Overseer _____

Trained By _____

Assimilator _____

Date Modified
12/16/93

DateCreated
12/8/93

MINISTRY POSITION DESCRIPTION

POSITION TITLE	MINISTRY	DEPARTMENT	M-LEVEL
SMALL GROUP LEADER	STUDENT IMPACT	YOUTH	3

Responsibilities

Group discipleship with 3-8 students with direction given by team director on selection of curriculum.

Passion for

Creating life-change in students and leading them to become fully-devoted followers of Christ.

Spiritual Gifts

Shepherding
Encouragement
Teaching

Personal Style

Energized ☒ People-Oriented
❑ Task-Oriented

Organized ☒ Structured
☒ Unstructured

Minimum Spiritual maturity

Stable/Growing

Talents/Skill/Abilities

Ability to spiritually nurture Christian high school students by relating on their level

Availability   ❑ Flexible

Mon	Tues	Wed	Thur	Fri	Sat	Sun
	R					

Regular Commitments

6:30-9:30p.m., Sunday

Length of Commitment

1 year

ADDITIONAL COMMENTS
Three weeks of training required to begin.

LOCATION

☒ Church   ❑ Home   ❑ Other:

SPECIAL NOTES

Membership Encouraged

Total Needed 22   Now Have 18   Openings 4

Staff Overseer _____

Trained By _____

Assimilator _____

Date Modified
12/16/93

DateCreated
12/8/93

MINISTRY POSITION DESCRIPTION

POSITION TITLE	MINISTRY	DEPARTMENT	M-LEVEL
USHER	USHER	SERVICE MIN.	1

Responsibilities

Serve at auditorium doors handing out bulletins & extending a warm welcome.

Assist in directing people to areas of need (classrooms, restrooms).

Tend exit doors.

Passion for

Providing a welcoming, warm and safe environment void of distractions so that they can hear God's truth through the events of the service.

Spiritual Gifts

Helps
Encouragement
Hospitality

Personal Style

Energized ☒ People-Oriented
❏ Task-Oriented

Organized ☒ Structured
☒ Unstructured

Minimum Spiritual maturity

New/Young

Talents/Skill/Abilities

Enjoy people
Able to think on their feet

Availability ☒ Flexible

Mon	Tues	Wed	Thur	Fri	Sat	Sun
						S
		S	S		S	

Regular Commitments

Length of Commitment

1 year

ADDITIONAL COMMENTS

LOCATION

❏ Church ☒ Home ❏ Other:

SPECIAL NOTES

Total Needed | 36   Now Have | 25   Openings | 11

Staff Overseer _____

Trained By _____

Assimilator _____

Date Modified
12/16/93

DateCreated
12/8/93

MINISTRY POSITION DESCRIPTION

POSITION TITLE	MINISTRY	DEPARTMENT	M-LEVEL
CONTACT TEAM HELPER	WOMEN'S MINISTRIES	ADULT MINISTRIES	2

Responsibilities

Help follow up with Network referrals and informational calls.

Passion for

Supporting and equipping women for life and ministry by encouraging them to take the next step in their personal growth (spiritually, relationally, emotionally, etc.).

Spiritual Gifts

Discernment
Administration
Hospitality

Personal Style

Energized ☒ People-Oriented
❑ Task-Oriented

Organized ☒ Structured
❑ Unstructured

Minimum Spiritual maturity

Stable/Growing

Talents/Skill/Abilities

Good with first impressions
Able to listen

Availability   ☒ Flexible

Mon	Tues	Wed	Thur	Fri	Sat	Sun

Regular Commitments

One-on-one meetings as scheduled

Length of Commitment

1 year

ADDITIONAL COMMENTS

LOCATION

❑ Church   ☒ Home   ❑ Other:

SPECIAL NOTES

Total Needed | 2   Now Have | 2   Openings | 0

Staff Overseer _____
Trained By _____
Assimilator _____

Date Modified
12/16/93

DateCreated
12/8/93

MINISTRY POSITION DESCRIPTION FORM

INSTRUCTIONS

(1) What is the M-category or ministry level of this position? M-Categories are a shorthand to describe the general minimum level of development or commitment required to complete this ministry position.

> **M1** - Seeker, available less than an hour/week, passion/gifts/style are untested/uncertain
>
> **M2** - New/Young believer, available 1-2 hours/week, passion/gifts/style need to generally fit the person and position
>
> **M3** - Stable/Growing believer, available 2-4 hours/week, passion/gifts/style need to specifically reflect the position
>
> **M4** - Leading/Guiding believer, available 4 + hours/week, passion/gifts/style are proven/affirmed, able to lead and develop people.

(2) What is the title of the position?

(3) What is the ministry that this position is a part of?

(4) What department of the church is this ministry in? (If you have them)

(5) What are the specific responsibilities of this position? Be as brief and descriptive as possible. (Leads and shepherds students by challenging them personally; leading a bimonthly small group and praying daily for them)

(6) What is the passion that someone needs to have to serve in this ministry or position?

(7) Considering the desired results of someone in this position, what spiritual gifts would be most appropriate to fulfill the responsibilities?

(8) Which style, if any, would be preferable if someone is going to stay motivated in this position over the long haul?

(9) What would be the "minimum" spiritual maturity level required to meet the expectations of this position?

---

(1) M-Category   M1   M2   M3   M4

(2) Position Title _____

(3) Ministry Name _____

(4) Department _____

(5) Responsibilities

_____

_____

_____

_____

(6) Passion _____

_____

(7) Spiritual Gifts _____

_____

(8) Personal Style

Energized: ___People-Oriented   *Organized:* ___Structured

___Task-Oriented   ___Unstructured

(9) Spiritual Maturity

___Seeker   ___Stable/Growing

___New/Young   ___Leading/Guiding

(10) Are there any specific talents or skills that might be helpful in order to effectively serve in this position?

(11) Using the key below, indicate the general times when these responsibilities can (or must) be accomplished by putting the letter in the appropriate time block.

(Flexible)–Serve at the volunteer's convenience - Check the box
(O) Optional–may serve at this time
(R) Required–must serve at this time
(S) Services–can serve before or after a service (which the volunteer attends)

(12) What other commitments are necessary? (Team meetings, training events, social events, etc.)

(13) What is the minimum length of time needed to effectively serve in this position? (Three months, six months, one year, etc.)

(14) Where can this ministry be accomplished?

(15) Are there any special requirements or restrictions that a volunteer needs to know about before being directed toward this position?

(16) How many people do you need in this position and how many do you presently have serving?

(17) Identify the full-time staff member responsible for this position.

(18) Who will be the initial person training the new volunteer?

(19) How will this volunteer be relationally connected to the team? Who will be providing care for them?

(20) Who is the person (Assimilator) within this ministry who is to be contacted by the volunteer?

(21) Is the Assimilator a volunteer or on staff?

(22) What is the Assimilator's phone number and where can they be reached?

(23) Are there any additional comments which might be helpful?

---

(10) Special Talents/Skills/Abilities

_____

_____

(11) Availability   ☐ **Flexible**

	Mon	Tue	Wed	Thu	Fri	Sat	Sun
am							
aft							
eve							

(12) Meetings and Regular Commitments
What?   *How Often?*
_____

(13) Length of Commitment
_____

(14) Location
____ Church   ____ Home   ____ Other: _____

(15) Special Notes
____ Membership Required   ____ By Invitation Only
____ Must Audition   ____ Other: _____

(16) Total Needed ____   **Now Have** ____

(17) Staff Overseer
_____

(18) Trained by
_____

(19) Team/Group Leader
_____

(20) Assimilator
_____

(21) ____ **Staff**   ____ **Volunteer**

(22) ____ **Work**   ____ **Home**   Phone (__) _____ -

(23) Additional Comments _____

NETWORK BENEFITS

A) Bible-based

B) Tested, proven, and effective

C) Realistically anticipates and allows for the "people factor"

D) Honest, inclusive, and participatory

E) Practical and repeatable

F) Based on years of experience in thousands of lives across denominational, regional, and cultural boundaries

G) You are not alone. Over 75,000 have used Network in hundreds of churches

H) Comprehensive volunteer identification and placement

I) Small group (meta-church) compatible: eight 45-minute sessions

J) Flexible formats (seminar, small group, retreat, Sunday school)

K) Interactive learning

L) Available in a kit or individual pieces. The kit includes:

> Implementation Guide
>
> Leader's Guide
>
> Participant's Guide
>
> Consultant's Guide
>
> Video: Network Drama Vignettes
>
> Video: Network Vision and Consultant Training
>
> Overhead Masters

M) Seminar audio cassettes also available

N) Average people will get above average success

O) It's simple, not necessarily easy, but it is simple

Network is not a product or a program, it is a process.
Network is not another ministry in the church, it is the way
you do church.

NETWORK IMPLEMENTATION SCHEDULE

This Sample Network Implementation Schedule shows how Network can be implemented in a year. A blank schedule for you to use at your church is provided on the pages of this guide immediately following this schedule. Use this schedule to plan for Network Implementation in your church. The Start Date is the day you start. The End Date is the date by which you plan to have your Network Ministry fully operational

Item *(Check each item when completed)*	Start Date ___/___ Month 1	Month 2	Month 3	Month 4
❑ I. Senior Leadership Commitment				
❑ Step 1: Form A Network Team				
❑ Step 2: Prepare The Network Proposal				
❑ Step 3: Present The Network Proposal To Senior Leadership				
❑ Step 4: Have Leadership Personally Experience Network				
❑ II. Ministry Preparation				
❑ Track A: Integrate Ministry Leaders Into Network				
❑ Step 1: Have The Ministry Leaders Personally				
Experience Network				
❑ Step 2: Facilitate Consultations Between Senior				
Leadership And Ministry Leaders				
❑ Step 3: Develop Network Ministry Position Descriptions				
❑ Track B: Identify and Train Additional Network Team Members				
❑ Step 1: Identify Additional Network Team Members				
❑ Step 2: Have Potential Network Team Members				
Personally Experience Network				
❑ Step 3: Select And Place Additional Network				
Team Members				
❑ Step 4: Have The New Network Team Members				
Prepare For Full Network Implementation				
❑ Step 5: Conduct Network Discovery Pilot				
❑ III. Network Implementation				
❑ Step 1: Have Senior Leadership Communicate Its				
Vision For Network To The Congregation				
❑ Step 2: Begin The Network Process				
❑ Step 3: Conduct Network Team Meetings				

NETWORK IMPLEMENTATION SCHEDULE

Month 5	Month 6	Month 7	Month 8	Month 9	Month 10	Month 11	End Date __/__ Month 12

Item *(Check each item when completed)*	Start Date __/__ Month 1	Month 2	Month 3	Month 4
❑ I. Senior Leadership Commitment	■	■	■	
❑ Step 1: Form A Network Team	▒			
❑ Step 2: Prepare The Network Proposal	▒	▒		
❑ Step 3: Present The Network Proposal To Senior Leadership		▒	▒	
❑ Step 4: Have Leadership Personally Experience Network			▒	
❑ II. Ministry Preparation			■	■
❑ Track A: Integrate Ministry Leaders Into Network			▒	▒
❑ Step 1: Have The Ministry Leaders Personally Experience Network				
❑ Step 2: Facilitate Consultations Between Senior Leadership And Ministry Leaders				
❑ Step 3: Develop Network Ministry Position Descriptions				
❑ Track B: Identify and Train Additional Network Team Members				
❑ Step 1: Identify Additional Network Team Members			▒	▒
❑ Step 2: Have Potential Network Team Members Personally Experience Network				
❑ Step 3: Select And Place Additional Network Team Members				
❑ Step 4: Have The New Network Team Members Prepare For Full Network Implementation				
❑ Step 5: Conduct Network Discovery Pilot				
❑ III. Network Implementation				
❑ Step 1: Have Senior Leadership Communicate Its Vision For Network To The Congregation				
❑ Step 2: Begin The Network Process				
❑ Step 3: Conduct Network Team Meetings				

NETWORK IMPLEMENTATION SCHEDULE - SAMPLE

Month 5	Month 6	Month 7	Month 8	Month 9	Month 10	Month 11	End Date __/__ Month 12

NETWORK MINISTRY BUDGET WORKSHEET

ITEM	AMOUNT
Revenue Items	
Funded by _____ budget	
Special gifts	
Participant tuition: $____ per person x ____ persons	
Other:	
Revenue Total	
Seminar Expenses	
Network Seminar Materials $____ per person x ____ persons	
Seminar Supplies (name tags, markers, etc.)	
Seminar refreshments (coffee, snacks, etc.)	
Seminar Publicity (printing, mailing cost, etc.)	
Other:	
Implementation Expenses	
Implementation Kit	
Consultant's Guides	
Consultant Training	
Supplies	
Other:	
Expense Total	
Revenue Total - Expense Total = Surplus (Deficit)	

Proposal   To implement Network at (*name of your church*) to get the right people in the right places for the right reasons.

What is Network?   Network is a proven and repeatable process of identifying and placing believers into meaningful places of service where they can be fruitful and fulfilled. It is a comprehensive approach that includes a 3-Step process of Discovery, Consultation, and Service. Network helps believers identify their God-given Passion, Spiritual Gifts, and Personal Style (*Servant Profile*) in order to understand and fulfill their ministry.

What are the benefits of Network?   This tested approach has many benefits:

It is biblical

It is a harmonious, integrated, and comprehensive system

It values people and their God-given uniqueness

It is realistic and practical

It is interactive, participatory, and inclusive

It can be used in a small group or seminar format

It increases motivation, involvement, and giving

How does Network work?   Network provides a simple 3-Step process:

1) The **Discovery** step (Step One) helps the believer to discover their God-given *Servant Profile* (Passion, Spiritual Gift, and Personal Style) through a series of eight 45-minute sessions. These step-by-step studies assist participants to better understand their place within God's design for serving in the church. A biblical foundation is presented and several self-scoring assessments are used to assist believers in their understanding.

2) A one-on-one **Consultation** (Step Two) follows the Discovery step. This personal interaction provides individualized attention for each volunteer in helping them find an appropriate place of service which reflects who God has made them to be (*Servant Profile*).

3) The goal of Network is **Service** (Step Three). Network's 3-step process moves people from the theology of the "priesthood of all believers" into the practical and God-honoring experience of it. Network facilitates the expression and application of our *Servant Profile* in the mission and ministry of the local church.

Network is not

Network is not another program for our church. Rather it is the practical introduction and reflection of a more biblical way of doing church. Network is not curriculum material for a program, it is a process for personal identification and ministry placement.

While Network will not solve all our recruiting needs, it is the best overall approach to get better and more motivated servants into meaningful places of ministry.

How would Network work in our church?

Network's Discovery sessions would be offered every other month. Consultations, placement, and follow-up would take place on the alternate months. Days and times would rotate throughout the year to provide a variety of opportunities for attendance.

Participation in the Network process will be strongly encouraged and emphasized, but will not be mandatory. We want to create a church-wide value of serving as another form of worship. We want people to act by need or desire to understand their God-given calling and purpose in life. Network offers critical insights to that understanding.

A Network Team will be identified and trained to develop and oversee the entire Network process.

The Network Team will support the sub-ministries of the church by identifying and referring qualified and motivated volunteers to their ministry. In cooperation with Ministry Leaders, the Network Team will put together ministry position descriptions on all the possible ways that people could serve in and through the church. This information will assist consultants in directing potential volunteers to places that reflect their *Servant Profile*.

Each participant attending the Discovery sessions will purchase their own materials ($). Each Participant's Guide contains all the needed assessments and notes they need for their personal discovery process.

Who can attend Network?

Network has not only been effective in helping believers to get started in ministry, but it has also proven to be an effective means of affirming those already serving in various ministry positions. Everyone can benefit by gaining a better understanding of their Passion, Spiritual Gifts, and Personal Style.

Implementing Network will require the church to commit staff, facilities, equipment, and a budget.

What does Network cost?

Fact: People who volunteer and give, give over twice as much as those who give and do not volunteer[1]

Staff: It is preferable that a full-time staff member be responsible for Network. Network may not be their only responsibility, but they are available to lead and relate the vision and values of Spiritual Gift-based, Passion-driven ministry.

Facilities: Office space will need to be allocated for the coordination and computerization of our people resources.

Equipment: A computer is critical to the building of Network's human resource database.

Budget: Implementation costs are estimated to be $_____
(This includes all the materials, database, and training)
Estimated annual budget will be $_____
(This includes promotional materials, forms, etc.)

When would the Network ministry begin?

It is estimated that it will take 10-12 months before we are in a position to present Network's Discovery sessions to the congregation. There are three phases to implementation:

Phase 1: Leadership Commitment

Senior Leadership needs to make a personal and organizational commitment to the Network process.

Phase 2: Ministry Preparation

Ministries in the church need to be integrated into Network, and additional Network Team members are identified and trained.

It includes: developing ministry position descriptions, training the Network Team and leading other ministry leaders through the process before "going public."

Phase 3: Network Implementation

The congregation is exposed to the vision of Network. They begin to be placed into service according to their *Servant Profile*.

It includes: presenting Discovery sessions and conducting consultations for the congregation.

We anticipate our first Network Discovery session to be

_____.

---

[1] Giving and Volunteering in the United States, 1992 edition, Independent Sector, 1828 L. Street NW, Washington DC 20036

NETWORK MINISTRY PROPOSAL WORKSHEET

The Goal of the Network Ministry at our church is:	
Network relates to our church's goals and vision as follows:	
The benefits to our church are:	
The Network Ministry will be organized and run by:	
The Network Ministry will be accountable to:	
The Network Ministry costs will be: (See budget worksheet)	
The Network Ministry will be funded by: (See budget worksheet)	
Network events will occur When:	
Network events will occur Where:	

NETWORK QUESTIONS AND ANSWERS

1. OUR PEOPLE ARE BUSY. CAN NETWORK'S DISCOVERY SESSIONS BE DONE IN ONE DAY?

The nature and content of the Network material requires some prayerful and honest reflection. Participants need time to reflect personally on the truths and principles being presented. It is not recommended to go through all eight sessions in a day, since people will not be able to adequately process the material.

2. WHAT ARE SOME OF THE ASSUMPTIONS UNDERLYING NETWORK?

A. Believers know they ought to serve.
B. Believers want to serve.
C. Believers do not know *how* they can serve.
D. Participants are not *required* to attend Network.
E. Everyone is self-motivated.
F. Everyone is a "10". . .somewhere.
G. God has designed each of us, and that design is unchangeable.
H. Each of us has a purpose for our lives which is partially revealed through our God-given Passion, Spiritual Gifts and Personal Style.
I. Believers want to be fruitful and fulfilled, making their unique contribution in a meaningful place of service.
J. Developing people builds ministry.
K. When people know who they are, they will find natural opportunities to express themselves in ministry.
L. Every believer is a minister, and therefore has a ministry.
M. Every church has all the resources it needs to do God's perfect will in that place at this time.
N. The goal is service.

3. DOES A PERSON'S PASSION CHANGE OVER TIME?

No. How we understand and express our Passion may vary throughout our life, but the essence of what most deeply moves us to action remains the same. Those who come to Christ later in their lives will often find what they care most about has its roots deep within them. Coming into a relationship with Jesus Christ gives many the deepest expression and most complete way in which to fulfill their God-given Passion. For an example, consider "Ted's Story" on page 64 in the Leader's Guide.

4. HOW DO NATURAL TALENTS AND SPIRITUAL GIFTS RELATE?

Natural talents are given by God to all people, Christian and non-Christian. They can be acquired skills or learned abilities. Spiritual Gifts are given by God to every believer in the body of Christ. They are given when we receive the Holy Spirit as a Christian. All that we have ought to be used for God's glory.

We need to be using our primary Spiritual Gifts in our ministry. Our talents may or may not find a specific opportunity for their expression. For example, a computer programmer (talent/skill) who has a Spiritual Gift of "Helps" or "Administration" might find their programming talent/skill a practical tool in using their Spiritual Gift. However, if this computer programmer has the Spiritual Gift of "Teaching" and a Passion for "children," this person ought to be teaching children.

In the same way, a nurse might have the Spiritual Gift of "Mercy" and use his or her nursing talents/skills in the context of a meaningful ministry. But if he or she has the Spiritual Gift of "Shepherding" with a Passion for "discipleship," this person probably ought to be leading a small group if he or she is to be fruitful and fulfilled.

5. WHAT IS A GIFT-MIX?

A gift-mix is a term used to describe those who have more than one Spiritual Gift. All believers have at least one, but some seem to have more than one. In those cases, the combination of gifts they have are called a "gift-mix." Their primary Spiritual Gift is complemented by other Spiritual Gifts which create a unique expression for ministry. For example, a gift-mix might have a primary Spiritual Gift of Teaching with complementing Spiritual Gifts of Knowledge and Wisdom. Giving might be complemented with Faith or Helps. Leadership might be complemented with Encouragement or Administration. The possible combinations are endless. God has given each of us those gifts which best suit our Personal Style, Passion, and purpose for our lives.

6. WHAT ARE "SPHERES OF SERVICE?"

There are three spheres of service in which we can use our Spiritual Gifts to minister.

A. Organizational (Structured/Ongoing)

These ministries meet regularly (weekly, monthly) and have been organized to serve and meet ongoing needs within a small group, the body, or community.

Serving in the Organizational Sphere leads to meaningful relationships and accountability. Our commitment to using our Spiritual Gifts is tested in the trenches of ongoing ministry, where we join forces with other servants in meeting a variety of needs. These regularly scheduled responsibilities reveal our need for God's strength and grace.

B. Projects (Periodic/Short-term)

These ministry opportunities meet special needs that arise periodically in the lives of those around us. Service is rendered until the task is completed, then the ministry team disbands.

Serving in the Projects Sphere stimulates greater creativity in the use of our Spiritual Gifts and encourages the spirit of servanthood. Just as financial giving includes both the regular tithe and special offerings, so ministry includes both regular and special tasks. Responding to these special tasks allows us to express our Spiritual Gifts in ways we do not do in regular service. Projects can thus "stretch us" and broaden the scope of our usefulness.

C. Promptings (Spontaneous/Personal)

These ministry opportunities are made available to each of us by the Holy Spirit. The Lord provides us with ways to use our Spiritual Gifts in personal and spontaneous expressions of grace.

Serving in the Promptings Sphere develops our Spiritual Gifts in the most profound way. In this context, no organizational structure of leadership guides the expression of our Spiritual Gifts. God-ordained opportunities to serve present themselves naturally as we cross paths with those who need the ministry of our specific Spiritual Gifts. As we obey the Spirit's promptings, we develop greater confidence in his guidance and find ourselves serving in increasingly unexpected and exciting ways.

The effective development of our Spiritual Gifts will encompass all three spheres of service: Organizational, Projects, and Promptings. Each sphere allows us unique expressions and insights for growth. Ministry satisfaction comes when we enjoy fruitfulness and fulfillment in each sphere. We must pursue them with diligence!

What can we definitely and specifically say about spiritual gifts as a result of our biblical understanding?

1) Every Christian has at least one spiritual gift.
   1 Peter 4:10

2) Unbelievers do not have spiritual gifts.
   1 Corinthians 12:27–28

3) No Christian has all the gifts.
   1 Corinthians 12:28–30

4) We cannot choose our gift(s).
   1 Corinthians 12:7–11

5) There is no spiritual gift which every Christian possesses.
   1 Corinthians 12:29–30

6) Believers will give an account to the Lord for how they. use their gift(s)
   1 Peter 4:10

7) Spiritual gifts indicate God's call and purpose for a believer's life.
   Romans 12:2–8

8) Gifts used without love do not accomplish God's intended purposes.
   1 Corinthians 13:1–3

9) Spiritual gifts are to edify the body of Christ.
   1 Corinthians 12:7

10) Gifts are for the common good.
    1 Corinthians 12:7

Vision

For the church to identify and place believers into meaningful places of service where they can be fruitful and fulfilled.

Values/Principles

1. We are commanded to serve. It's biblical (Galatians 5:13). Serving is not an option. We are called to serve as an act of obedience.

2. Serving is a form of worship. It's God-honoring (Romans 12:1). We ascribe honor and worship to God through our tithes, songs, words, and deeds.

3. Serving is a form of stewardship. It's responsible (1 Peter 4:10). God holds us accountable, measuring our fruitfulness according to the grace and the gifts we express.

4. Developing people builds ministry. It's investing (Ephesians 4:11–12). Attention is given to the person, not the position, emphasizing the "who" before considering the "what."

5. People need meaningful places of service. It's purposeful (Romans 12:6). Ministry motivation results from the perception of significance an individual attaches to a particular task.

6. People have something to give and something to receive. It's interdependence (1 Peter 4:10; 1 Corinthians 12:7). Each servant has something to offer and something to receive from the body of Christ. These relationships are interdepedent.

7. Everyone is a "10" somewhere. It's unique (Ephesians 4:16). Ineffective ministry results from the right people in the wrong positions. Making your unique contribution makes youm a "10" somewhere.

8. People need to know who they are. It's revelational (John 13:3; Psalm 26:2). Increasing one's self-understanding increases the chance to discover the place of unique contribution.

9. People are in process and therefore need a process. It's developmental (1 Corinthians 12:1; I Timothy 4:14). Life is a journey of growing experiences. Helpful "snapshots" indicate where a growing person is presently.

10. The goal is to eliminate the laity. It's revolutional (1 Corinthians 12:27). We are all the people of God. Clergy/laity paradigms and attitudes hinder the Holy Spirit's power with the lives of his people. We are all called to be ministers and therefore have a ministry.

THE NEXT STEP

NAME: _____

The next step for me is to contact the following ministries and complete the final step of Network: Service.

The consultant and I agree the ministry to consider at this time would be:

M:

Ministry A _____

Contact person _____

Phone _____

Ministry B _____

Contact person _____

Phone _____

Ministry C _____

Contact person _____

Phone _____

My Consultant was _____
Phone _____ Date _____

PERSONAL

Name _____ Network Sessions Month /Year _____/_____

Address _____ Apt# _____

City _____ State _____ Zip _____

Home Phone (_____) _____ Work Phone (_____) _____

Birth Date _____ ❏ Male ❏ Female

FAMILY

Marital Status: ❏ Single ❏ Married

Spouse's name: _____ Birthdate: _____

Children names:

_____ ❏ M ❏ F Birthdate: _____
_____ ❏ M ❏ F Birthdate: _____
_____ ❏ M ❏ F Birthdate: _____
_____ ❏ M ❏ F Birthdate: _____
_____ ❏ M ❏ F Birthdate: _____
_____ ❏ M ❏ F Birthdate: _____

CHURCH

When did you start attending the church? Month/Year: _____/_____
Are you a member?   ❏ Yes   ❏ No
Small Groups: ❏ I am in one (Leader's name _____)
                          ❏ I would like to be in one
                          ❏ I used to be in one (Leader's name _____)
                          ❏ Other: _____

CURRENT MINISTRY INVOLVEMENT

Which of the following ministries are you now involved in?   ❏ None
Ministry _____ Leader _____
Ministry _____ Leader _____
List other ministries or community groups outside the church in which you are involved:
Ministry/Group _____
Ministry/Group _____

PAST MINISTRY INVOLVEMENT

Which of the following ministries
have you been involved in in the past?   ❏ None
Ministry _____ Leader _____
Ministry _____ Leader _____
List other ministries or community groups outside the church in which you have been involved:
Ministry/Group _____
Ministry/Group _____

SERVANT PROFILE AND CONSULTATION SUMMARY

**Complete Prior To
Your Consultation**

I have a **Passion** for:

1. _____
2. _____

My **Spiritual Gifts** are:

1. _____
2. _____
3. _____

Shaded Area To Be Completed By Consultant

Passion

1. _____
2. _____

Spiritual Gifts

1. _____
2. _____
3. _____

My **Personal Style** is:
- ❏ People-Oriented/Structured
- ❏ Task-Oriented/Structured
- ❏ People-Oriented/Unstructured
- ❏ Task-Oriented/Unstructured

I would describe my **spiritual maturity** as:
- ❏ Seeker
- ❏ Stable/growing believer
- ❏ New/young believer
- ❏ Leading/guiding believer

I would describe my current **availability** as:
- ❏ Limited, 1-2 hrs
- ❏ Significant, 4+ hrs
- ❏ Moderate, 2-4 hrs
- ❏ Not sure

I would like to know more about the following ministries:

_____

_____

_____

The following ministries were identified as possible places of service: M Category: _____

A. _____ B. _____ C. _____

Consultant: _____ Phone: _____

Comments: _____

_____

_____

EMPLOYMENT

❑ I am employed   ❑ Self Employed   ❑ Unemployed

Name of Company _____

Title/Responsibilities _____

Product or service _____

EDUCATION

❑ High School   ❑ Some College   ❑ Other
❑ College   ❑ Masters Degree
❑ Doctorate   ❑ Professional Degree

SPIRITUAL JOURNEY

How did you come to know Christ personally? How do you maintain your relationship?

_____
_____
_____
_____
_____
_____
_____
_____
_____
_____
_____
_____
_____
_____
_____
_____
_____
_____
_____
_____
_____

In addition to your *Servant Profile*, please go through each area, carefully marking the boxes which indicate talents or skills in which you have proven ability. In other words, indicate areas in which you have demonstrated a reasonable amount of confidence and competence. You are not making a commitment to serve in any area where you check a box, but we would like to have this information on file in case of special needs. Be honest and fair in your self-evaluation.

Professional Services
- ❏ Mental Health
- ❏ Social Work
- ❏ Financial
- ❏ Dental
- ❏ Medical
- ❏ Chiropractic
- ❏ Legal
- ❏ Accounting
- ❏ Bookkeeping
- ❏ Taxes
- ❏ Nursing
- ❏ Landscaping
- ❏ Carpet Cleaning
- ❏ Window Washing
- ❏ Engineer:
- ❏ Lifeguard
- ❏ Counseling
- ❏ Career Counseling
- ❏ Unemployment
- ❏ Day Care Director
- ❏ Law Enforcement
- ❏ Personnel Mgr.
- ❏ Public Relations
- ❏ Advertising
- ❏ Television: _____
- ❏ Radio
- ❏ Computer Prog.
- ❏ Paramedic/EMT
- ❏ Systems Analyst
- ❏ Journalist/Writer
- ❏ _____

Art
- ❏ Layout
- ❏ Photography
- ❏ Graphics
- ❏ Multi-Media
- ❏ Typesetting
- ❏ Crafts
- ❏ Artist
- ❏ Banners
- ❏ Decorating
- ❏ _____

Teaching or Assisting
- ❏ Preschool
- ❏ Elementary
- ❏ Junior High
- ❏ Senior High
- ❏ Single Adults (18-29)
- ❏ Single Adults (30+)
- ❏ Couples
- ❏ Men's Group
- ❏ Women's Group
- ❏ Tutoring
- ❏ Learning Disabled
- ❏ Researcher
- ❏ Aerobics
- ❏ Budget Counselor
- ❏ _____

Mechanical
- ❏ Copier Repair
- ❏ Diesel Mechanic
- ❏ Auto Mechanic
- ❏ Small eng. Repair
- ❏ Mower Repair
- ❏ Machinist
- ❏ _____

Office Skills
- ❏ Typing (40+ wpm)
- ❏ Word Processing
- ❏ Receptionist
- ❏ Office Manager
- ❏ Data Entry
- ❏ Filing
- ❏ Mail Room
- ❏ Library
- ❏ Transcription
- ❏ Shorthand
- ❏ _____

Missions
- ❏ Missionary
- ❏ Evangelism
- ❏ _____

Theatrical
- ❏ Actor/Actress
- ❏ Poet
- ❏ Dance
- ❏ Mime
- ❏ Puppets
- ❏ Clowning
- ❏ Audio Production
- ❏ Sound/Mixing
- ❏ Lighting
- ❏ Set Construction
- ❏ Set Design
- ❏ Stage Hand
- ❏ Script Writer
- ❏ _____

Construction
- ❏ General Contractor
- ❏ Architect
- ❏ Carpenter: General
- ❏ Carpenter: Finish
- ❏ Carpenter: Cabinet
- ❏ Electrician
- ❏ Plumbing
- ❏ Heating
- ❏ Air Conditioning
- ❏ Painting
- ❏ Papering
- ❏ Masonry
- ❏ Roofing
- ❏ Telephones
- ❏ Drywall Finishing
- ❏ Concrete
- ❏ Carpet Installer
- ❏ Interior Design
- ❏ Drafting
- ❏ _____

Working With
- ❏ Handicapped
- ❏ Hearing Impaired (Signing)
- ❏ Incarcerated
- ❏ Learning Disabilities
- ❏ Nursing Homes/Shut-Ins
- ❏ Hospital Visitation
- ❏ Meals on Wheels
- ❏ Housing for Homeless
- ❏ _____

General Help
- ❏ Cashier
- ❏ Child Care
- ❏ Customer Service
- ❏ Food Service
- ❏ Gardening
- ❏ Building Maintenance
- ❏ Grounds Maintenance
- ❏ Transportation
- ❏ Snow Removal
- ❏ Catering/Cooking
- ❏ Weddings
- ❏ Bookstore
- ❏ Tape Duplication
- ❏ Plant Care (Indoor)
- ❏ ports Official
- ❏ Sports Instructor
- ❏ _____

Musical
- ❏ Choir Director
- ❏ Choir
- ❏ Soloist
- ❏ Instrument
- ❏ Composer
- ❏ Arranger
- ❏ Piano Tuner
- ❏ _____

Are there any other products, specific resources, skills, interests, talents, abilities, or unique opportunities (example: permitted access to specialized purchasing/discounts for the church) that you would like to offer to the church?

_____

I understand that this information will be made available only to responsible and appropriate staff and ministry leaders at this church.

Signature: _____ Date: _____

PERSONAL RESOURCES SURVEY — 1
SAMPLE

PERSONAL

Name _____Nick Stuart_____ Network Sessions Month /Year _Dec. / 1993_

Address __P. O. Box 3188_____ Apt# _____

City_____Barrington_____ State __IL__ Zip _____

Home Phone (_708_) _765-0070_____ Work Phone (____) _____

Birth Date _____ ☒ Male ❑ Female

FAMILY

Marital Status: ☒ Single ❑ Married

Spouse's name: _____ Birthdate: _____

Children names:

_____	❑ M	❑ F	Birthdate: _____
_____	❑ M	❑ F	Birthdate: _____
_____	❑ M	❑ F	Birthdate: _____
_____	❑ M	❑ F	Birthdate: _____
_____	❑ M	❑ F	Birthdate: _____
_____	❑ M	❑ F	Birthdate: _____

CHURCH

When did you start attending the church? Month/Year: _____April / 1992_____

Are you a member? ❑ Yes ☒ No

Small Groups:
  ❑ I am in one (Leader's name _____)
  ☒ I would like to be in one
  ❑ I used to be in one (Leader's name _____)
  ❑ Other: _____

CURRENT MINISTRY INVOLVEMENT

Which of the following ministries are you now involved in? ☒ None

Ministry _____ Leader _____

Ministry _____ Leader _____

List other ministries or community groups outside the church in which you are involved:

Ministry/Group _____

Ministry/Group _____

PAST MINISTRY INVOLVEMENT

Which of the following ministries
have you been involved in in the past? ☒ None

Ministry _____ Leader _____

Ministry _____ Leader _____

List other ministries or community groups outside the church in which you have been involved:

Ministry/Group _____

Ministry/Group _____

SERVANT PROFILE AND CONSULTATION SUMMARY

**Complete Prior To
Your Consultation**

I have a **Passion** for:
1. *Drama*
2. _____

My **Spiritual Gifts** are:

1. *Giving*
2. *Creative Communication*
3. *Evangelism*

Shaded Area To Be Completed By Consultant
Passion
1. _____
2. _____
Spiritual Gifts
1. _____
2. _____
3. _____

My **Personal Style** is:
- ❏ People-Oriented/Structured
- ❏ Task-Oriented/Structured
- ☒ People-Oriented/Unstructured
- ❏ Task-Oriented/Unstructured

I would describe my **spiritual maturity** as:
- ❏ Seeker
- ❏ Stable/growing believer
- ☒ New/young believer
- ❏ Leading/guiding believer

I would describe my current **availability** as:
- ❏ Limited, 1-2 hrs
- ❏ Significant, 4+ hrs
- ☒ Moderate, 2-4 hrs
- ❏ Not sure

I would like to know more about the following ministries:

Drama Team

Information Center

In Touch

The following ministries were identified as possible places of service: M Category: _____

A._____ B._____ C._____

Consultant: _____ Phone: _____

Comments: _____
_____
_____

EMPLOYMENT

❏ I am employed   ☒ Self Employed   ❏ Unemployed

Name of Company ___*Stuart Communications*___

Title/Responsibilities ___*Owner*___

Product or service ___*Cellular Telephone Distributor*___

EDUCATION

❏ High School   ❏ Some College   ❏ Other
☒ College   ❏ Masters Degree
❏ Doctorate   ❏ Professional Degree

SPIRITUAL JOURNEY

How did you come to know Christ personally? How do you maintain your relationship?

My life was lacking, and I didn't know where to turn. I started attending the seeker service at our church, and the message really made sense. After tiptoeing around for a couple months, I struck up a conversation with a couple folks.

We went out for lunch, and they explained the Gospel to me. Not long after that I received Christ as my savior. I attend both the Sunday seeker service, and the mid-week service for believers.

I have also been reading through the Bible, and try to spend at least a few minutes a day in focused prayer. I plan to take Impact Evangelism the next time it is offered at our church.

In addition to your *Servant Profile*, please go through each area, carefully marking the boxes which indicate talents or skills in which you have proven ability. In other words, indicate areas in which you have demonstrated a reasonable amount of confidence and competence. You are not making a commitment to serve in any area where you check a box, but we would like to have this information on file in case of special needs. Be honest and fair in your self-evaluation.

Professional Services
- ❏ Mental Health
- ❏ Social Work
- ❏ Financial
- ❏ Dental
- ❏ Medical
- ❏ Chiropractic
- ❏ Legal
- ❏ Accounting
- ❏ Bookkeeping
- ❏ Taxes
- ❏ Nursing
- ❏ Landscaping
- ❏ Carpet Cleaning
- ❏ Window Washing
- ❏ Engineer:
- ❏ Lifeguard
- ❏ Counseling
- ❏ Career Counseling
- ❏ Unemployment
- ❏ Day Care Director
- ❏ Law Enforcement
- ❏ Personnel Mgr.
- ❏ Public Relations
- ❏ Advertising
- ❏ Television: _____
- ❏ Radio
- ❏ Computer Prog.
- ❏ Paramedic/EMT
- ❏ Systems Analyst
- ❏ Journalist/Writer
- ❏ _____

Art
- ❏ Layout
- ❏ Photography
- ❏ Graphics
- ❏ Multi-Media
- ❏ Typesetting
- ❏ Crafts
- ❏ Artist
- ❏ Banners
- ❏ Decorating
- ❏ _____

Teaching or Assisting
- ❏ Preschool
- ❏ Elementary
- ❏ Junior High
- ❏ Senior High
- ❏ Single Adults (18-29)
- ❏ Single Adults (30+)
- ❏ Couples
- ❏ Men's Group
- ❏ Women's Group
- ❏ Tutoring
- ❏ Learning Disabled
- ❏ Researcher
- ❏ Aerobics
- ❏ Budget Counselor
- ❏ _____

Mechanical
- ❏ Copier Repair
- ❏ Diesel Mechanic
- ❏ Auto Mechanic
- ❏ Small eng. Repair
- ❏ Mower Repair
- ❏ Machinist
- ❏ _____

Office Skills
- ❏ Typing (40+ wpm)
- ❏ Word Processing
- ❏ Receptionist
- ❏ Office Manager
- ❏ Data Entry
- ❏ Filing
- ❏ Mail Room
- ❏ Library
- ❏ Transcription
- ❏ Shorthand
- ❏ _____

Missions
- ❏ Missionary
- ❏ Evangelism
- ❏ _____

Theatrical
- ☒ Actor/Actress
- ❏ Poet
- ❏ Dance
- ☒ Mime
- ❏ Puppets
- ❏ Clowning
- ❏ Audio Production
- ❏ Sound/Mixing
- ❏ Lighting
- ☒ Set Construction
- ☒ Set Design
- ❏ Stage Hand
- ❏ Script Writer
- ❏ _____

Construction
- ❏ General Contractor
- ❏ Architect
- ❏ Carpenter: General
- ❏ Carpenter: Finish
- ❏ Carpenter: Cabinet
- ❏ Electrician
- ❏ Plumbing
- ❏ Heating
- ❏ Air Conditioning
- ❏ Painting
- ❏ Papering
- ❏ Masonry
- ❏ Roofing
- ❏ Telephones
- ❏ Drywall Finishing
- ❏ Concrete
- ❏ Carpet Installer
- ❏ Interior Design
- ❏ Drafting
- ❏ _____

Working With
- ❏ Handicapped
- ❏ Hearing Impaired (Signing)
- ❏ Incarcerated
- ❏ Learning Disabilities
- ❏ Nursing Homes/Shut-Ins
- ❏ Hospital Visitation
- ❏ Meals on Wheels
- ❏ Housing for Homeless
- ❏ _____

General Help
- ❏ Cashier
- ❏ Child Care
- ❏ Customer Service
- ❏ Food Service
- ❏ Gardening
- ❏ Building Maintenance
- ❏ Grounds Maintenance
- ❏ Transportation
- ❏ Snow Removal
- ❏ Catering/Cooking
- ❏ Weddings
- ❏ Bookstore
- ❏ Tape Duplication
- ❏ Plant Care (Indoor)
- ❏ ports Official
- ❏ Sports Instructor
- ❏ _____

Musical
- ❏ Choir Director
- ❏ Choir
- ❏ Soloist
- ❏ Instrument
- ❏ Composer
- ❏ Arranger
- ❏ Piano Tuner
- ❏ _____

Are there any other products, specific resources, skills, interests, talents, abilities, or unique opportunities (example: permitted access to specialized purchasing/discounts for the church) that you would like to offer to the church?

_____

I understand that this information will be made available only to responsible and appropriate staff and ministry leaders at this church.

Signature: ___*Nick Stuart*_____   Date: ___*Decmber 18, 1993*___

Administration

Opportunities are available for people with a wide variety of skill levels to do office work including: data entry, typing, mailings, copying, answering phones, and the like.

Adopt-A-Bed

The Adopt-A-Bed program requires the regular weeding and keeping of the many flower beds and trees. An individual or family "adopts" a particular area of the grounds for their weekly care. You may tend to your specific "bed" anytime each week. Those who enjoy gardening or working with their hands might consider this ministry.

Artists

Artistic people are able to express themselves through a variety of formats, including banners, original art, and special designs. Individuals with experience in stage/set design are needed throughout various ministries within the church.

Buddy

This ministry provides sensitive and mature role models through big brother/big sister type relationships for the children of single-parent families.

Careers

The unemployed and those seeking career advancement or transition can find help and support through the Careers ministry. Compassionate people are needed who are skilled in areas of career development, encouragement, counseling, leadership, and human resources.

Cars

This team of automotive mechanics regularly meets to use their skills and abilities to repair the cars of those who are struggling financially. They seek to provide basic, reliable transportation for those in need.

Card and Letter Writers

People write cards and letters of encouragement to those who are in hospitals, nursing homes, and those struggling with grief from death. Significant ministry happens as caregivers serve through the written word.

Caseworkers

The goal of this team is to move an individual or family from a point of crisis to a point of stability by providing guidance and referrals to those facing severe stress due to financial need.

Community Care Teams

The Community Care Teams are a visitation ministry that brings compassion and assistance for the sick and hurting into the hospital and home.

Defenders

This ministry is for people with a heart for evangelism and who are able to "give an answer to everyone" (1 Peter 3:15) who ask tough questions about the faith including atheists, agnostics, and those in cults and other religions. Members meet to sharpen their ability to respond to these intellectual challenges in order to effectively serve as a referral team to the evangelism ministry as well as the wider church body.

Disciplemaking Groups

These groups are designed to disciple believers, help bring people together for closer fellowship, and provide an environment where each person can continue to mature in their personal relationship with Jesus Christ. Qualified leaders help individuals gain further insight into God's Word through group discussion and help members make personal application in everyday life.

Drama Team

The drama team provides opportunities for creative expression of the arts during the weekend and some mid-week services. Men and women with an interest in acting, writing, or assisting with props and costumes are encouraged to participate. Auditions for actors and actresses are held annually.

Evangelism

The primary functions of the evangelism ministry are to train our believers in relational evangelism (through the four-week Evangelism Seminar offered on a monthly basis) and to harness, equip, and deploy those with gifts or passions in this area.

Exodus

Exodus is a ministry to ex-offenders and supports families of the incarcerated. Long-term caring relationships are established with individuals and families. Encouragement and guidance are provided to the prisoner and his re-entry into society and the family.

Family Life

Administrative support for the Family Life Ministries (Rebuilders, Marriage, and Single Parent Family Ministries) is provided through several dedicated teams of volunteers. Telephone work, computer work, and a variety of administrative projects are opportunities for service. People with gifts of Administration, Helps, Encouragement, or Mercy are welcome.

Flute Ensemble

The flute ensemble prepares the atmosphere for worship through playing preludes for the various services once a month. Auditions are held throughout the year. Players must be at high school proficiency level or higher.

Good Sense

Good sense educates people in biblically-based personal applications of money management primarily through one-on-one budget counseling. Additional education is provided through "Principles of Money Management" seminars in budgeting, biblical foundations, and through teaching seminars in the sub-ministries. Counselors must be discerning encouragers who can sensitively discuss a counselee's personal finances and who model sound money management.

Grounds

The beautiful atmosphere of our church is carefully manicured by several dedicated teams of workers. There are a wide variety of opportunities for those who enjoy serving outdoors year round (tree trimming, landscaping, lawn care, snow removal). More technical skills are needed also (diesel mechanic, vehicle maintenance, mower repair).

Hearing Impaired

Two teams meet the needs of this ministry. First, interpreters are needed to communicate services to the hearing impaired so they are able to access the many ministries of the church. Second, hearing impaired volunteers are needed for assisting in evangelism, administration, Bible studies, and event planning.

Heritage

The elderly residing in area nursing homes and retirement centers are ministered to through the Heritage ministry. There are sing-alongs, Bible studies, worship services, musical performances, and informal times for individual caring. Meaningful relationships are developed through regular sharing and visitation.

In Touch

The In Touch ministry utilizes people from a variety of ministry areas who are evangelistically sensitive and have a heart for visitors and seekers. Team members respond each week to the weekend program tear-off cards that have been turned in. Contacts are made on the phone and are followed-up, when appropriate, with a personal meeting. The goal of the team is to answer questions about the ministries of the church, make newcomers feel welcomed, and to seek to encourage people spiritually.

Information Center

Friendly and helpful people provide assistance to visitors having questions about and of the church's ministries. General brochures and specific program information are available through any of the Lobby Information Centers. Those serving must be well-informed and familiar with our church and its programs.

Medical Ministry

Through a variety of service opportunities the Medical Ministry seeks to provide areas of service for health care providers who wish to use their professional training, talents, and gifts in assisting the poor and oppressed on a global scale. As a part of International Ministries, the medical team is committed to ministry that addresses all areas of human need: physical, social, economic, emotional, and spiritual. The scope of this ministry is both local and international.

Moms

The Moms group is an encouragement ministry to women with preschool children. Peer support and fellowship groups give insight and relief to mothers. Activities throughout the year include play days, holiday craft night, and a fall brunch. Women are encouraged through a monthly publication for moms, *Doodles and Daydreams*.

Network

Network is committed to helping those who are seeking to serve the church find a meaningful place of service. Regular sessions are taught, followed by personal one-on-one consultations which are designed to guide the individual to a ministry which is an expression of who God made them to be. Network involves consultants, encouragers, administrators, follow-up callers, and data-entry.

Oasis Ministry

This ministry provides a haven for children from single-parent families. As the single parents participate in support opportunities, God's love and care are communicated to their children through activities, relationships, and teaching.

Office Assistants

Daytime and evening office help serve the needs of various ministries through word processing, filing, photo copying, preparing mailers, typing, etc.

Pathfinders

This ministry provides understanding, support, and encouragement to those who are coping with chronic afflictions (cancer, diabetes, multiple sclerosis, and others), and to family or friends who are caregivers to them.

Prayer Team

This ministry meets regularly to pray for and follow-up with persons who request prayers by calling or writing our pastoral care department.

Promiseland

Promiseland is a ministry that helps the family in their attempt to lay a spiritual foundation that, in God's timing, will lead every child into a personal relationship with Jesus Christ. During the weekend services, people can serve directly with children (e.g., by giving care or leading a small group), use creative communication gifts, or assist the adults, enabling them to serve effectively. Help during the week consists of giving administrative assistance in preparation for weekend services.

Rebuilders

Rebuilders provides biblical insight and relational support to anyone who has gone through marital breakdown in order to bring them to a God-honoring resolution. Both restoration of marriages and recovery from divorce are purposes pursued by those in attendance. Volunteers are needed with gifts of Shepherding, Teaching, Mercy, Wisdom, Administration, Helps, Hospitality, Wisdom, and Faith.

Refugee Resettlement

International Ministries partners with World Vision and various ethnic churches in the support of refugees arriving in the area from around the world. Refugees escaping political, religious, and ethnic persecution usually arrive in the U. S. with little more than the clothes on their backs. Support from International Ministries for these refugees can include food, clothing, furniture, housewares, and economic and transportation assistance. Individuals with the gift of Helps or the desire to relate cross-culturally are needed in very practical ways.

Short-Term Teams

Through International Ministries members can use their gifts, abilities, and resources to serve for one or two weeks in other parts of the world. The result of this service is an expanded vision of God's activity, particularly among the poor, while practically assisting other ministries and churches in work projects and other identified needs. Whether you have practical skills or just a willing desire to serve, all individuals can make a significant impact. Training is provided for all those selected to participate on a team.

Single Parent Families

The Single Parent Family ministry seeks to meet the needs of single parents and their children by meeting together for mutual encouragement and support in ways which honor God. Spiritual growth, individual psychological health, and family stability are promoted through retreats, activities, and periodic seminars.

Sonlight Express

Junior High students (grades 6-8) meet each Saturday morning for high energy competition, video, small group discussion, and a relevant message. Adults serve in a variety of capacities: small group leaders, team directors, competition directors, production, music/drama, and the Task Force. Time, love, and a passion for junior high students are required for participation in Sonlight Express.

Special Friends

This team ministers to the spiritual needs of the developmentally disabled in the community along with their family members by seeking out ways to serve and facilitate them through their involvement in various ministries.

Student Impact

Student Impact allows adults who have a passion for high school youth to train students to improve their caring skills so that the students may be more effective in reaching peers who are struggling, but seeking to fit in personally, emotionally, and spiritually. Spiritual gifts of Teaching, Leadership, or Encouragement are desired.

Urban Ministry

International Ministries' Urban Ministry provides cross-cultural opportunities in the metropolitan area. Through selected partnerships, Urban Ministry provides service in such areas as tutoring, construction/repair, general labor, English as a Second Language (ESL), and soup kitchen help. Individuals who have a desire to serve the impoverished or in a cross-cultural setting are encouraged to participate.

Ushers

Ushers care for people as they enter the auditorium. As a bulletin is received and a person finds a seat, ushers are available to answer questions, and provide direction. When a special need arises, ushers respond in ways that cause as little disturbance as possible to the service.

Wedding Ministry

The Wedding Ministry has been developed to assist engaged couples while planning their wedding. Volunteers are needed as Wedding Consultants to work closely with each couple, coordinating the final details of their wedding day.

Women's Ministries

Women's Ministries provides a variety of opportunities throughout the year for the women of the church. Whether in the home or marketplace, Women's Ministries is committed to being supportive through Bible studies, discipleship groups, workshops, an annual Spring Luncheon, and Breakfasts for Working Women. Other opportunities include working with our publications for women which are a monthly verse calendar and a quarterly "Journal."

Worship Team

The worship team leads congregational worship during mid-week services. Gifted vocalists with the ability to sing in groups and convey inspirational worship are encouraged to participate. Auditions are held on a need basis.

SAMPLE NETWORK TRACKING FORM

Session Date	# Registered	# Attended	# Signed up for consultation	# Completing consultation	# Serving

BIBLICAL CONTEXT

Network integrates servanthood, scripture, and stewardship themes in a basic and overall understanding of ministry.

DISCOVERY PROCESS

It provides the process through which believers can move from where they are to where they should be in their ministry through the local church.

ASSESSMENTS

Multiple assessments and probing questions assist believers in identifying who God has made them to be and indicate possible areas for service.

SERVANT PROFILE

Each participant is able to articulate their *Servant Profile* (Passion, Spiritual Gifts, and Personal Style).

PERSONALIZED

Quality materials have been developed which value the volunteer.

PLACEMENT STRATEGY

Network not only teaches, but consults and refers volunteers to places of possible service. There is a complete integrated support system.

MOTIVATIONAL

Network enlivens the believers to fulfill their call and purpose in life.

PROVEN

Network has been experienced by thousands of believers in churches around the world.

APPEALS TO DIVERSE AUDIENCES

Network benefits every believer (old/young, men/women, city/rural, etc.) and bridges many differences (denominational lines, geographical regions, cultural boundaries, large and small church dynamics, etc.) because it has been developed upon biblical principles.

IMPLEMENTATION PROCESS

Vision, values, and strategy are complemented with training and support materials to implement Network in the local church.

BENEFICIAL

Network is one of the most significant "gifts" with which you can serve your church. It is the gift that enables others to keep on giving!

BIBLIOGRAPHY

Background
The New Reformation, Greg Ogden, Zondervan
Pouring New Wine Into Old Wineskins, Aubrey Malphurs,
   Baker Books

General
Serving One Another, Gene Getz, Victor Books
The New Reformation, Greg Ogden, Zondervan
Unleashing the Church, Frank Tillapaugh, Regal Books
Unleashing Your Potential, Frank Tillapaugh, Regal Books
Partners In Ministry, James Garlow, Beacon Hill Press of Kansas City
The Body, Chuck Colson, Word Publishing
What Color Is Your Parachute?, Richard Bolles, Ten Speed Press
Improving Your Serve, Charles Swindoll, Word Publishing

Passion
The Truth About You, Arthur Miller/Ralph Mattson, Ten Speed Press

Spiritual Gifts
Spiritual Gifts, Bobby Clinton, Horizon House
Spiritual Gifts, David Hocking, Promise Publishing
Team Ministry, Larry Gilbert, Church Growth Institute
Spiritual Gifts Can Help Your Church Grow, Peter Wagner, Regal Books
Finding (and Using) Your Spiritual Gifts, Tim Blanchard, Tyndale House
Discovering Spiritual Gifts, Paul Ford, Fuller Institute

Personal Style
Please Understand Me, David Keirsey/Marily Bates, Prometheus
   Nemesis Book Co.
Understanding How Others Misunderstand You, Ken Vogues/Ron
   Braund, Moody
The Delicate Art of Dancing With Porcupines, Bob Phillips,
   Regal Books

Other Resources
Serving Sessions, Bill Hybels, Seeds Tapes
   (Willow Creek Community Church)

Network Ministry Support
Willow Creek Association
P.O. Box 3188
Barrington, IL 60011-3188
Phone: 708/765-0070
Fax: 708/765-5046

Network Ministries International
27355 Betanzos
Mission Viejo, CA 92692
800-588-8833

Willow Creek Resources® is a publishing partnership between Zondervan Publishing House and the Willow Creek Association®. Willow Creek Resources® includes drama sketches, small group curricula, training material, videos, and many other specialized ministry resources.

Willow Creek Association® is an international network of churches ministering to the unchurched. Founded in 1992, the Willow Creek Association® serves churches through conferences, seminars, regional roundtables, consulting, and ministry resource materials. The mission of the Association is to assist churches in reestablishing the priority and practice of reaching lost people for Christ through church ministries targeted to seekers.

For conference and seminar information please write to:

Willow Creek Association
P. O. Box 3188
Barrington, Illinois 60011-3188